Improving Transition Assistance for Reserve Component Members

AGNES GEREBEN SCHAEFER, MARIA MCCOLLESTER, MOLLY DUNIGAN, MICHELLE GRISÉ, KATHERINE KUZMINSKI

Prepared for the Office of the Secretary of Defense
Approved for public release; distribution is unlimited

RAND NATIONAL DEFENSE RESEARCH INSTITUTE

For more information on this publication, visit **www.rand.org/t/RRA2071-1**.

About RAND

The RAND Corporation is a research organization that develops solutions to public policy challenges to help make communities throughout the world safer and more secure, healthier and more prosperous. RAND is nonprofit, nonpartisan, and committed to the public interest. To learn more about RAND, visit www.rand.org.

Research Integrity

Our mission to help improve policy and decisionmaking through research and analysis is enabled through our core values of quality and objectivity and our unwavering commitment to the highest level of integrity and ethical behavior. To help ensure our research and analysis are rigorous, objective, and nonpartisan, we subject our research publications to a robust and exacting quality-assurance process; avoid both the appearance and reality of financial and other conflicts of interest through staff training, project screening, and a policy of mandatory disclosure; and pursue transparency in our research engagements through our commitment to the open publication of our research findings and recommendations, disclosure of the source of funding of published research, and policies to ensure intellectual independence. For more information, visit www.rand.org/about/research-integrity.

RAND's publications do not necessarily reflect the opinions of its research clients and sponsors.

Published by the RAND Corporation, Santa Monica, Calif.
© 2023 RAND Corporation
RAND® is a registered trademark.

Library of Congress Cataloging-in-Publication Data is available for this publication.

ISBN: 978-1-9774-0980-5

Cover: From Sgt. 1st Class Anthony L. Taylor and gorodenkoff/Getty Images.

About This Report

Military-to-civilian transitions are a broad set of experiences that occur when active and reserve component members separate from the military, when reserve component members switch from extended active duty back to reserve duty, and when service members retire. Senate Report (S.R.) 114-255 directed the U.S. Department of Defense (DoD) to conduct research on the transition experiences of *reserve component members* (i.e., members of both the Reserves and National Guard), make recommendations to the Senate Armed Services Committee on how to better meet the transition needs of this population, or alternatively, suggest a transition program specifically designed for the reserve component. In this report, we support DoD in meeting these S.R. 114-255 requirements by (1) identifying the transition needs of reserve component members who meet the eligibility requirements to participate in the DoD's Transition Assistance Program (TAP), as well as the needs of transitioning reserve component members who do not meet current eligibility requirements; (2) assessing how to best address the needs of these transitioning reserve component members (e.g., considerations for TAP policy, content, or program delivery methods); and (3) recommending how to optimally deliver and improve TAP for reserve component members.

The research reported here was completed in June 2022 and underwent security review with the sponsor and the Defense Office of Prepublication and Security Review before public release.

RAND National Security Research Division

This research was sponsored by the Office of the Secretary of Defense and conducted within the Forces and Resources Policy Program of the RAND National Security Research Division (NSRD), which operates the National Defense Research Institute (NDRI), a federally funded research and development center sponsored by the Office of the Secretary of Defense, the Joint Staff, the Unified Combatant Commands, the Navy, the Marine Corps, the defense agencies, and the defense intelligence enterprise.

For more information on the RAND Forces and Resources Policy Program, see www.rand.org/nsrd/frp or contact the director (contact information is provided on the webpage).

Acknowledgments

We would like to extend our thanks to numerous offices and entities throughout the Office of the Secretary of Defense and the various military services for their support over the course of this study. We also benefited from the contributions of our RAND colleagues.

Jeffrey Wenger provided input throughout the study. Daniel Ginsberg, Lisa Harrington, Tom Bush, and Jim Powers provided helpful peer reviews of this report. Most importantly, we thank the many reserve component members who graciously shared with us their transition experiences and perspectives on how to improve transitions for reserve component members.

We could not have done this work without them, but we assume full responsibility for the objectivity, accuracy, and analytic integrity of the work presented here.

Summary

Issue

Military-to-civilian transitions are a broad set of experiences that occur when active and reserve component members separate from the military, when reserve component members switch from extended active duty back to reserve duty, and when service members retire. Senate Report (S.R.) 114-255 directed the U.S. Department of Defense (DoD) to conduct research on the transition experiences of *reserve component members* (i.e., members of both the Reserves and National Guard), make recommendations to the Senate Armed Services Committee on how to better serve the transition needs of this population, or alternatively, suggest a transition program specifically designed for the reserve component. In this report, we support DoD in meeting these S.R. 114-255 requirements by (1) identifying the transition needs of reserve component members who meet the eligibility requirements to participate in the DoD's Transition Assistance Program (TAP), as well as the needs of transitioning reserve component members who do not meet current eligibility requirements; (2) assessing how to best address the needs of these transitioning reserve component members (e.g., considerations for TAP policy, content, or program delivery methods); and (3) recommending how to optimally deliver and improve TAP for reserve component members.

Approach

We approached this study using a qualitative methodology, consisting of targeted literature reviews, informational discussions with transition service providers, and focus groups with reserve component members. In June 2018, the RAND Corporation's Human Subjects Protection Committee determined that this research was not research involving human subjects, and DoD concurred with that determination. Our literature review focused on findings from government documents and the academic literature on the needs of transitioning reserve component members and the degree to which DoD's TAP addresses the needs of transitioning reserve component members.

We also held informational discussions with non-TAP reserve component transition service providers to better understand the transition needs of reserve component members and to elicit their suggestions for ways to better address those needs.[1] We took notes during all informational discussions and focus groups, then coded this information to identify transitioning reserve component member needs, resources that reserve component members have used during their transitions, which aspects of TAP were most helpful to them, which aspects

---

[1] Non-TAP service providers are providers who are not affiliated with the DoD's TAP. These include other DoD and nongovernmental service providers.

were least helpful to them, and their recommendations for how to improve transition support to reserve component members. We next synthesized the findings from the literature and policy reviews with those from our informational discussions with service providers and focus groups to identify (1) unmet needs for transitioning reserve component members; (2) the impact of current reserve component TAP requirements on individuals and units; and (3) potential improvements to TAP, specifically for reserve component members. Finally, drawing from our findings, we developed recommendations on how to improve TAP's effectiveness in addressing reserve component members' transition needs.

Key Findings

The following key findings emerged from our analysis of the literature reviews, informational discussions with non-TAP transition service providers, and focus groups with reserve component members:

- Reserve component members have transition needs in seven key areas.
- TAP focuses on active component members' transition needs and does not adequately address reserve component members' transition needs.
- The 180-day active duty requirement results in reserve component members taking TAP multiple times with diminishing returns.
- The timing and location of TAP are problematic for reserve component members.

The concerns about TAP arose during focus groups from late 2019 to early 2022. Over the course of this period of the study, DoD began to reformat TAP based upon requirements included in the National Defense Authorization Act for Fiscal Year 2019.[2] The changes were intended to provide service members with a TAP experience more tailored to their individual circumstances. As with the past iteration of TAP, the services may deploy and manage TAP in their own ways, as long as their members meet the established programmatic deadlines.[3] Directly prior to publication of this report, the study team learned that the services have already begun to deploy these authorities and address the report's recommendations, including, in some cases, waiving the TAP attendance requirement for members who have already completed the course after 180 days of active duty service and providing one-on-one counseling. The results of those changes are still being assessed.

---

[2] Public Law 115-232, John S. McCain National Defense Authorization Act for Fiscal Year 2019; Section 552, Improvements to Transition Assistance Program, August 13, 2018.

[3] Department of Defense Instruction 1332.35, *Transition Assistance Program (TAP) for Military Personnel*, U.S. Department of Defense, September 6, 2019, pp. 13–14.

Reserve Component Members Have Transition Needs in Seven Key Areas

We found that reserve component members have transition needs in seven key areas: (1) navigating employment challenges and accessing benefits, (2) navigating education-related challenges and accessing benefits, (3) navigating health care–related challenges and accessing benefits, (4) navigating financial challenges, (5) identifying and accessing retirement benefits, (6) accessing local transition services, and (7) navigating the timing of the TAP course. This finding provides insight into the unique transition needs of reserve component members and the areas in which DoD can focus its efforts to assist transitioning reserve component members.

TAP Focuses on Active Component Transition Needs and Does Not Adequately Address Reserve Component Transition Needs

We found that many reserve component members feel that, in its current form, TAP does not adequately address reserve component transition needs. Instead, it focuses primarily on active component members who are preparing to separate from the military and embark on a civilian career for the first time. Many reserve component members (especially more-seasoned members) find that the material presented during TAP is not relevant to reserve component members and does not address the unique transition challenges that reserve component members face as they switch between their military and civilian careers.

The 180-Day Active Duty Requirement Results in Reserve Component Members Taking TAP Multiple Times with Diminishing Returns

We found that many focus group participants had taken TAP several times during their careers—some as many as seven times—because of the statutory requirement to take TAP after being on active duty orders for 180 days or more. Many focus group participants expressed frustration that they had to repeatedly take TAP and that each time they took it, it had diminishing returns. This issue is the root of other reserve component members' concerns related to TAP, such as TAP is repetitive, TAP is a one-size-fits-all model and is too rigid, and more-senior service members should be able to opt out of parts of or all of TAP.

Timing and Location of TAP Are Problematic for Reserve Component Members

We found that the timing (especially when TAP occurs at the end of a deployment) and the location of TAP (especially at a demobilization site far from home) are problematic for reserve component members. Many focus group participants told us that when reserve component members are taking TAP while they are demobilizing at an active component installation at the end of their deployment, they are not fully focused on TAP because they need to focus on completing their mission and they want to return to their families.

Recommendations

As Congress considers ways in which to improve TAP to better address the transition needs of reserve component members, we offer the following recommendations:

- change the automatic requirement to take TAP after 180 days of active duty service
- make TAP more customizable and flexible to meet individual transition needs
- ensure reserve component members have access to one-on-one counseling
- consider developing a Reserve Component–focused TAP course
- connect reserve component members to the broader support network of state and local transition resources through TAP
- collect regular feedback on TAP so continuous improvements can be made to the program.

We briefly discuss each of these recommendations in the sections that follow.

Change the Automatic Requirement to Take TAP After 180 Days of Active Duty Service

The current requirement mandates that reserve component members take TAP every time they are on active duty for 180 days or more, which leads to them taking TAP multiple times over a short period, even if they have already taken TAP or are simply returning to their previous job. We recommend that this 180-day requirement for reserve component members to take TAP be revised. An alternative requirement that might better meet the needs of reserve component members would be to require all members returning from their first prolonged time on active duty orders to take TAP and then allow members to opt in to take relevant sections of TAP in the future as their careers progress. A requirement for all reserve component members to take a short refresher TAP course every five years or so may also be helpful to ensure members stay up to date on changes in benefits.

Make TAP More Customizable and Flexible to Meet Individual Transition Needs

Our discussions with reserve component members highlight the degree to which they want TAP to be more customizable and flexible in order to meet individual members' transition needs. We recommend that DoD consider permitting reserve component members tailor their TAP experience by allowing them to opt into those courses and access information that they and a counselor or commander determine are needed most and to opt out of courses and receiving information that they do not need at various points in the progression of their military and civilian careers.

Ensure Reserve Component Members Have Access to One-on-One Counseling

Although access to one-on-one counseling is a requirement in the newest version of TAP, many of the reserve component members with whom we spoke had never had a one-on-one counseling session. Such a counseling option could identify any challenges that individuals have early and help them plan for their transitions and access the benefits that they are eligible for during those transitions. It would also address reserve component members' concern that they currently "get lost in the system" and do not know how to access their various benefits.

Consider Developing a Reserve Component–Focused TAP Course

One of the options that DoD asked us to explore in our study is whether there is a need to establish a separate TAP course for reserve component members. Our findings compel us to recommend that DoD consider developing such a Reserve Component–focused TAP course. Significant differences in transition needs between active and reserve component members warrant separate courses. We recommend that this course focus on issues that typically challenge reserve component members after returning from prolonged active duty, such as issues related to pay, access to health care and other support services, and health insurance and other benefits. If the development of a separate course is found to be unfeasible, we recommend that DoD add at least one component to the current TAP curriculum that focuses on the unique transition challenges and needs of reserve component members.

Connect Reserve Component Members to the Broader Support Network of State and Local Transition Resources Through TAP

During our focus groups, one of the dominant themes we heard from reserve component members is that they would like to access transition resources closer to the communities in which they live for greater convenience and relevance; however, we also heard that very few TAP participants had been connected to those state and local resources through the program or other transition service providers. We recommend that DoD help link transitioning reserve component members to this broader web of support resources in a manner similar to other initiatives to support service members and military families, such as Joining Forces and the Military Spouse Employment Partnership, to enable reserve component members to access DoD, U.S. Department of Labor, and state and local resources closer to home. DoD does not need to "do it all," so by connecting reserve component members to this broader support network, DoD could expand its efforts to help transitioning reserve component members and provide them with services closer to home.

Collect Regular Feedback on TAP So Continuous Improvements Can Be Made to the Program

When we asked focus group participants whether they had had an opportunity to provide feedback on TAP after taking the course, a surprisingly large number told us that the RAND focus group was the first time they had such an opportunity. Therefore, we recommend that DoD administer regular opportunities to provide feedback on TAP. Without this feedback, it is difficult to identify the extent to which TAP is effectively addressing the transition needs of reserve component members and opportunities for improving TAP.

Contents

CHAPTER 1

Introduction

Background and Study Purpose

Military-to-civilian transitions are a broad set of experiences that occur when service members separate from the military, when reserve component members switch from extended active duty to reserve component duty, and when service members retire.[1] Previous research has demonstrated that some reserve component members experience difficult transitions back to civilian life after prolonged active military service of 180 consecutive days or more. In its 2014 report entitled *Transitioning Veterans: Improved Oversight Needed to Enhance Implementation of Transition Assistance Program*, the U.S. Government Accountability Office (GAO) recommended that the Secretary of Defense increase efforts to measure the performance of and evaluate the results of the Transition Assistance Program (TAP). GAO acknowledged that reserve component members have unique transition needs that the TAP curriculum may need to address.[2] In addition, the 2016 Senate Report (S.R.) 114-255 directed the U.S. Department of Defense (DoD) to conduct research on the transition experiences of *reserve component members* (i.e., members of both the Reserves and National Guard), make recommendations to the Senate Armed Services Committee on how to better meet the transition needs of this population, or alternatively, suggest a transition program specifically designed for the Reserve Component.[3]

In this report, we support DoD in meeting these S.R. 114-255 requirements by (1) identifying transition needs for reserve component members who meet the eligibility requirements to receive TAP, as well as the needs of transitioning service members who do not meet current eligibility requirements; (2) assessing how to best address the needs of these transitioning

---

[1] Many reserve component members spend time within a "gray area," in which they have completed their 20 years of service to acquire retirement benefits, but they have yet to reach the age for retirement. When they reach retirement age, they often need support identifying which retirement benefits they are eligible for and how to access them.

[2] GAO, *Transitioning Veterans: Improved Oversight Needed to Enhance Implementation of Transition Assistance Program*, GAO-14-144, March 2014a.

[3] U.S. Senate, *National Defense Authorization Act for Fiscal Year 2017 Report (to Accompany S. 2943)*, U.S. Government Publishing Office, S.R. 114-255, May 18, 2016.

reserve component members (e.g., considerations for TAP policy, content, or program delivery methods); and (3) recommending how to optimally deliver and improve TAP for reserve component members.

Study Objectives and Approach

The objectives of this study were to identify the transition needs of reserve component members and provide recommendations on how DoD's transition programs can better meet the needs of reserve component members. We approached these objectives through a qualitative methodology, consisting of focused literature reviews, informational discussions with transition service providers, and focus groups with reserve component members. Our literature review focused on findings from government documents and the academic literature on the needs of transitioning reserve component members and the degree to which DoD's TAP addresses those needs.

We also held informational discussions with non-TAP reserve component transition service providers to better understand the transition needs of reserve component members and to elicit suggestions from them for ways to better address those needs.[4] These informational discussions and literature reviews then informed focus groups consisting of reserve component members who have and have not completed the TAP curriculum. These focus groups gave us a better understanding of reserve component members' transition experiences and transition needs.

We took notes during all informational discussions and focus groups, then coded this information to identify transitioning reserve component member needs, current resources available to meet those needs, which aspects of TAP were most helpful, which aspects were least helpful, and their recommendations for how to improve transition support to reserve component members. We derived the main takeaways from these coded data and reported the most prevalent themes and responses from our focus group discussions. We then synthesized the findings from the literature and policy reviews, service provider discussions, and focus groups to identify (1) unmet needs for transitioning reserve component members; (2) the impact of current reserve component TAP requirements on individuals and units; and (3) potential improvements to TAP, specifically for reserve component members. Key findings include the effects of the pace, timing, and access to TAP on reserve component members.

---

[4] Non-TAP service providers are providers who are not affiliated with DoD's TAP. These include other DoD and nongovernmental service providers.

Organization of This Report

The remainder of this report is organized into five chapters. Chapter 2 provides background and context regarding the history and structure of TAP. In Chapter 3, we synthesize observations and perspectives from our literature reviews and non-TAP transition service providers regarding the needs of transitioning reserve component members. Chapters 4 and 5 present findings from our focus groups with reserve component members: first regarding their transition needs and the resources they have used during their transitions, then regarding their perspectives on TAP and how to improve it. Chapter 6 presents our findings and recommendations for improving transition support, and specifically TAP, to better meet the needs of reserve component members. Readers can find protocols for our discussions with non-TAP service providers and our focus groups with reserve component members in Appendixes A and B, respectively.

CHAPTER 2

TAP Background

Two laws established the framework for the current version of TAP. First, the fiscal year (FY) 1991 National Defense Authorization Act (NDAA) included a provision for the establishment of support programs for separating military service members. The FY 1991 NDAA outlined a list of services and benefits that included pre-separation counseling on transition topics and benefits, employment assistance, relocation and housing assistance, medical benefits, and federal and law enforcement recruitment and preference benefits. The law stipulated that TAP participation was to be voluntary in nature and meant to provide opportunities, not mandatory requirements. These protections and services are now codified in U.S. Code; the efforts to implement this law became known as TAP.[1]

In 2011, Congress passed the VOW (Veterans Opportunity to Work) to Hire Heroes Act, which sought to improve the employment rate of veterans through various education, training, and employment support options. The act mandated that all service members who have been on active duty for 180 days or more participate in TAP as part of an overall plan to increase service members' chances for post-separation employment. The law also refined the employment assistance provided to transitioning service members by requiring agencies and departments to determine which military skills could be applicable in various types of civilian positions. The law further required service members to thoroughly consider their professional skills and how to apply them in the civilian marketplace.[2]

Because of shifting needs of the military and transitioning service members, TAP received an overhaul in 2013. The revised version of the program sought to improve upon existing transition assistance to better meet the wide variety of service members' needs. Six partnering agencies were included in the 2013 version of TAP and continue to provide services today: DoD, the U.S. Department of Veterans Affairs (VA), the U.S. Department of Labor (DOL), the Office of Personnel Management, the U.S. Small Business Administration (SBA), and the U.S. Department of Education. These six agencies signed a memorandum of understanding (MOU) and interagency agreement that determined and delineated specific programmatic

---

[1] U.S. Code, Title 10, Chapter 58, Benefits and Services for Members Being Separated or Recently Separated, Sections 1141–1153, January 3, 2012a.

[2] Public Law 112-56, VOW to Hire Heroes Act, November 21, 2011.

responsibilities.[3] These obligations are stipulated in federal regulations under which the program presently operates. The current version of TAP is available for all service members and their spouses, including members of the Reserves and National Guard, if the service member has completed a minimum of 180 consecutive days of active duty in a deployment.[4]

After we began our research for this study, DoD reformatted TAP based on requirements included in the FY 2019 NDAA. These changes were intended to provide service members with a TAP experience more tailored to their individual circumstances. The 2019 version of TAP provided many of the same elements as the previous iteration that was in place since 2013; however, the 2019 version of TAP shortens the time required to complete the entire program. As outlined in DoD Instruction 1332.35, all service members transitioning out of the military must take three days of initial courses (described in more detail below),[5] which shortened the original five-day TAP core curriculum. Additionally, in the 2019 version of TAP, service members could take one of the additional two-day focused workshops or tracks offered, depending on their level of transition preparedness.[6] If a TAP counselors deems a service member to be unprepared for transition during their initial counseling session, the service member is required to attend one of these additional workshops. Those service members who are determined to be prepared for their transition may or may not choose to attend an additional workshop.[7] These options allow for more service members to take advantage of the two-day workshops than before, when the workshops were offered as optional add-ons to the original five-day core curriculum.[8] As with the past iteration of TAP, the services may

---

[3] The U.S. Department of Homeland Security is also included in the MOU as a representative for Coast Guard service members, but it does not provide TAP services.

[4] Code of Federal Regulations, Title 32, National Defense; Chapter I, Office of the Secretary of Defense; Subchapter D, Personnel, Military and Civilian; Part 88, Transition Assistance for Military Personnel; Section 88.2, Applicability and Scope; DoD, "Memorandum of Understanding Among the Department of Defense, Department of Veterans Affairs, Department of Labor, Department of Education, Department of Homeland Security (United States Coast Guard), United States Small Business Administration, United States Office of Personnel Management Regarding the Transition Assistance Program for Service Members," January 31, 2014; DoD, "Interagency Statement of Intent Among the Department of Defense, Department of Veterans Affairs, Department of Labor, Department of Education, United States Office of Personnel Management, and United States Small Business Administration Regarding the Redesigned Transition Assistance Program for Separating Service Members," August 15, 2013.

[5] DoD *Instruction 1332.35, Transition Assistance Program (TAP) for Military Personnel*, September 26, 2019, pp. 22–23.

[6] There are four two-day tracks or workshops that service members may take.

[7] DoD *Instruction 1332.35, Transition Assistance Program (TAP) for Military Personnel, U.S. Department of Defense*, September 26, 2019; Natalie Gross, "TAP Is Getting a Makeover This Year. Here's What You Need to Know," *Military Times*, June 28, 2019.

[8] According to a 2017 GAO report, fewer than 15 percent of service members opted to take one of the additional two-day workshops when the TAP core curriculum programming lasted five days (GAO, *Transitioning Veterans: DOD Needs to Improve Performance Reporting and Monitoring for the Transition Assistance Program*, GAO-18-23, November 2017, p. 23).

deploy and manage TAP in their own ways, as long as their members meet the established programmatic deadlines.[9]

Current TAP Structure

The current version of TAP, which includes changes made in response to requirements in the FY 2019 NDAA, employs a curriculum-based program that targets overall post-separation outcomes for service members. The program applies a modular style curriculum "designed to provide service members with the resources, tools, services, and skill-building training needed to meet career readiness standards (CRS)."[10] CRS are "a set of career preparation activities Service members must complete to depart from active-duty and be considered 'career ready.'"[11] TAP offers in-person courses at military installations across the country and overseas and through an online portal for those members unable to attend in person.[12] The current version of TAP consists of four main elements: (1) individual initial counseling, (2) pre-separation counseling, (3) core curriculum with workshop option, and (4) capstone review.[13]

TAP Individual Initial Counseling

Service members' official start in the transition process occurs with individualized initial counseling, in which they are assigned a TAP counselor. During these one-on-one sessions, counselors assist service members in completing their self-assessment and developing their individual transition plan (ITP).[14] Both of these activities help service members walk through different aspects of their post-military life (e.g., employment, finances, health) and determine areas in which they may need assistance.

---

[9] DoD Instruction 1332.35, 2019, pp. 13–14.

[10] DoD TAP, "About DoD TAP," webpage, undated-a.

[11] DoD TAP, "Career Readiness Standards Overview," fact sheet, undated-d.

[12] DoD Instruction 1332.35, 2019, pp. 26–27, 51.

[13] The required timing of participating in TAP varies by service members' transition status. If a transitioning service member is retiring, transition assistance should begin as soon as possible within two years of the anticipated retirement date. If a service member is separating but not through retirement, transition assistance should begin as soon as possible within a year of the anticipated separation date. If separation or retirement is unanticipated, or in the case of reserve component members who are demobilized under circumstances in which timelines cannot be upheld, transition assistance must begin as soon as possible within the remaining period of service. See DoD Instruction 1332.35, 2019, p. 23.

[14] The ITP is a self-assessment tool that assists service members in identifying their unique needs and goals for transitioning out of the military. See DoD, "Transition Assistance Initial Self-Assessment Worksheet," 2022b.

TAP Pre-Separation Counseling

This second element of TAP offers more-detailed information on the processes and requirements for exiting military service. This one-on-one counseling covers information that, by law, service members must know and includes material on benefits, entitlements, and resources to help with their transition to civilian life.[15] For active duty service members, pre-separation counseling must start no later than 365 days prior to their planned separation date.[16]

TAP Core Curriculum with Two-Day Track Option

After the first two counseling sessions, service members progress to the heart of TAP—the core curriculum. The core curriculum takes three to five days to complete, depending on the evaluation of an individual service member's needs during the initial counseling period.[17] The core curriculum consists of three courses: (1) the DoD Transition Day course, (2) the VA Benefits and Services course, and (3) the DOL Employment Fundamentals of Career Transition course. We provide an overview of each of these courses in the subsequent sections.

DoD Transition Day Course

The first day of the core curriculum consists of three subprograms.[18] The first subprogram, Managing Your (MY) Transition, provides service members with an overview of transitioning from military-to-civilian life in general and of the TAP courses to follow. This overview covers the following topics: personal and family transition concerns, cultural differences and considerations between military and civilian workplaces, transition-related stressors, effective communication strategies, and general resources available to service members and their families. The second subprogram develops and reviews service members' Military Occupational Code Crosswalk. During this crosswalk exercise, service members compile their experience and skills developed while in the military, translate their military experience and skills into marketable language used in civilian occupations, and identify gaps in their training or experience needed to meet their career goals. The third subprogram, Financial Planning for Transition, educates service members on how their transition will affect their financial circumstances and aids in developing or updating financial plans. This course covers the following topics: changes in income, taxes, health care costs, and new expenses; processes to calculate military-to-civilian income shifts; and the expected costs of living for intended or existing home locations. Although the course broadly covers financial aspects for all tran-

---

[15] U.S. Code, Title 10, Chapter 58, Section 1142, Pre-separation Counseling; Transmittal of Certain Records to Department of Veterans Affairs, January 3, 2012b; DoD, *Pre-Separation Counseling Resource Guide*, October 2021, p. 9.

[16] DoD TAP, "Initial and Pre-Separation Counseling," webpage, undated-e; DoD, 2021, pp. 8–9.

[17] This description reflects intended changes to the implementation of TAP courses initiated in 2019.

[18] DoD TAP, "TAP Curriculum," webpage, undated-g.

sitioning service members, some specific sections address the financial needs of reserve component members, such as Reserve Component–specific health care and retirement pay considerations.[19]

VA Benefits and Services Course

The second day of the TAP core curriculum provides an overview of VA benefits and programs. In this class, service members learn which programs and benefits they are eligible for, depending on their status and years of service. The VA benefits course covers such topics as disability benefits; memorial and burial benefits; education and economic support; housing benefits; and health care options to address physical, emotional, and mental needs. The course uses real-life case studies and service members' stories to illustrate how benefit eligibility can differ depending upon a service member's unique circumstances. The VA benefits course covers Reserve Component–specific information, including eligibility requirements for VA benefits and services.[20]

DOL Employment Fundamentals of Career Transition Course

The third day of the TAP core curriculum focuses on career options for transitioning service members. Organized by DOL, the Employment Fundamentals of Career Transition course introduces service members to the tools and resources available to evaluate their career options, understand civilian employment, and learn about the civilian employment process.[21]

TAP Two-Day Track Options

Upon completion of the three-day core TAP curriculum, some service members may attend one of four optional workshops (also referred to as "two-day tracks").[22] During initial counseling, TAP counselors determine which service members would benefit from further assistance provided in one of these workshops. Army, Navy, and Marine Corps members deemed in need of additional assistance select one of the workshops based upon their career goals. The Air Force permits any service member, regardless of their initial counseling assessment, to choose whether to attend a workshop.[23]

Each of the two-day workshops address one topic: education, vocation, employment, or entrepreneurship. The Managing Your (MY) Education helps service members determine which higher education option best suits their educational goals and needs. This education workshop is designed for service members considering college or graduate education for the

---

[19] DoD, *2022 TAP Curriculum: Financial Planning for Transition*, 2022a, pp. 30, 36, and 54.

[20] DoD TAP, undated-g; VA, *VA Benefits and Services Participant Guide*, undated.

[21] DoD TAP, undated-g.

[22] DoD TAP, "Two-Day Tracks," webpage, undated-h.

[23] Gross, 2019.

first time and covers such topics as choosing a field of study, selecting a school, the admission process, and financial support options.[24]

DOL's Vocational Training Track focuses on a personalized career development assessment of service members' interests and abilities. This workshop is geared toward careers that may not require post-secondary education (i.e., jobs that require licenses and certifications rather than academic degrees). Drawing on their personal assessment, service members acquire tailored job recommendations that align with their skill sets and experiences. Additional topics that are addressed during the workshop include the civilian job market, education, apprenticeships, certifications, and licensure requirements.[25]

The DOL Employment Workshop provides more in-depth information on the topics that are covered during the DOL Employment Fundamentals of Career Transition course in the TAP core curriculum. It addresses such topics as in-depth training for interviews, creating effective resumes, and using emerging technology for networking and identifying job opportunities.[26]

The SBA's Entrepreneurship Track, known as Boots to Business, introduces service members to the skills, knowledge, and resources needed to launch a business. The workshop includes access to additional online coursework to further service members' skills and knowledge. The workshop also connects service members to program partners and other veteran programs run by SBA for networking and guidance opportunities.[27]

TAP Capstone Review

The capstone review serves as the final step of TAP. During the capstone review, each service member has their ITP reviewed by their commander, a designee, or both. The review ensures that service members have all the information that they need to successfully transition from military to civilian life and to meet the TAP career readiness standards. If, during the review, the commander or designee determines that the service member requires additional information or support, they will arrange for a personal handover from DoD to another agency to provide such assistance.[28]

---

[24] DoD TAP, undated-h.

[25] DoD TAP, undated-h.

[26] DoD TAP, undated-h.

[27] DoD TAP, undated-h.

[28] DoD TAP, "Capstone," webpage, undated-b.

CHAPTER 3

Identifying the Transition Needs of Reserve Component Members

To identify the transition needs of reserve component members, we used a multifaceted qualitative methodology consisting of focused literature reviews, informational discussions with transition service providers, and informational discussions with two of the services to get a sense of retiring reserve component members' needs. This chapter presents the findings from each facet of our approach, followed by a summary of all our findings. We used these findings to develop our focus group protocols for reserve component members (see Appendix B).

Findings from Our Targeted Literature Review

As part of our research design, we initially conducted a review of relevant government policies and documents and academic research that identify reserve component members' transition needs. This review proved especially critical in shaping our discussions with non-TAP transition service providers, as well as our focus group discussions with reserve component members. From this review, one major point became apparent: Congress, other government officials, and researchers agree that reserve component members have unique transition needs. However, many of the documents that we reviewed pointed to the need for additional research to determine exactly what those needs are and how they might be addressed.

Congress has shown sustained interest in the military-to-civilian transition of service members, with a heightened level of concern starting in 2012 and continuing through to present day. This interest has included the oversight of transition services, multiple redesigns of TAP, and the implementation of the redesigned TAP in 2019. Congressional hearings and reports have also noted the desire to know more about how the military-to-civilian transition specifically affects reserve component members. Congress has acknowledged that reserve component members might require alternative or additional transition assistance, but it has offered few specific suggestions about what those particular needs might be or how they might be addressed by TAP.[1] This consistent Congressional attention has prompted GAO to

---

[1] U.S. House of Representatives, Back from the Battlefield: DOD and VA Collaboration to Assist Service Members Returning to Civilian Life, Joint Hearing Before the Committee on Armed Forces and Com-

evaluate TAP, its implementation, and its performance management.[2] Our review of GAO's reports identified two areas of TAP-related challenges for reserve component members: geography and course timing.[3]

Our review of academic research provided further insights into the transition needs of reserve component members. The majority of relevant academic research often focuses upon veterans' issues more broadly, with only a few distinct examinations of reserve component members as a separate population. Thus, drawing upon both veteran- and Reserve Component–related academic research, we identified four additional areas of transition challenges and needs—employment, education, health, and finances—which, combined with the two TAP-related challenges and needs, produced an initial list of reserve component transition challenges and needs. We discuss each of these areas in the subsequent sections.

Reserve Component Members Face Unique Employment Challenges and Needs During Transition

We found that reserve component members face specific employment challenges. Many reserve component members lose their jobs either during or after their deployments because employers often cannot or will not permit them to hold their positions during their time away. Although the Uniformed Services Employment and Reemployment Rights Act (USERRA) protects service members from such treatment, employers still terminate service members'

---

mittee on Veterans' Affairs, U.S. Government Printing Office, July 25, 2012a; U.S. House of Representatives, *Examining the Re-Design of the Transition Assistance Program (TAP): Hearing Before the Subcommittee on Economic Opportunity of the Committee on Veterans' Affairs*, U.S. Government Printing Office, September 20, 2012b; U.S. Senate, *Is Transition Assistance on Track? Hearing Before the Committee on Veterans' Affairs*, U.S. Government Publishing Office, December 15, 2015; U.S. House of Representatives, *Lowering the Rate of Unemployment for the National Guard and Reserve: Are We Making Progress? Hearing Before the Subcommittee on Economic Opportunity of the Committee on Veterans' Affairs*, U.S. Government Printing Office, March 14, 2013a; U.S. House of Representatives, *A Review of the Transition Assistance Program (TAP): Hearing Before the Subcommittee on Economic Opportunity of the Committee on Veterans' Affairs*, U.S. Government Publishing Office, January 27, 2015a; U.S. House of Representatives, *Status of Implementation of the Requirements of the VOW Act and the Recommendations of the Presidential Veterans Employment Initiative Task Force for the DoD Transition Assistance Program—Goals, Plans, and Success (GPS): Hearing Before the Subcommittee on Military Personnel of the Committee on Armed Services*, U.S. Government Printing Office, April 24, 2013b; U.S. House of Representatives, *Transition Assistance Program—A Unity of Effort: Hearing Before the Subcommittee on Military Personnel of the Committee on Armed Services*, U.S. Government Publishing Office, October 28, 2015b; U.S. House of Representatives, *Oversight Plans for All House Committees*, 110th Congress–115th Congress, U.S. Government Publishing Office, 2007–2017.

[2] GAO, *Military and Veterans' Benefits: Enhanced Services Could Improve Transition Assistance for Reserves and National Guard*, GAO-05-544, May 2005; GAO, 2014a; GAO, *Veterans Affairs: Better Understanding Needed to Enhance Services to Veterans Readjusting to Civilian Life*, GAO-14-676, September 2014b; GAO, 2017; GAO, *Military Personnel: DOD's Transition Assistance Program at Small or Remote Installations*, GAO-21-104608, July 2021.

[3] GAO, 2005, pp. 21–24; GAO, 2014a, pp. 26–28.

employment in direct violation of USERRA.[4] While some reserve component members must deal with unemployment, most often, reserve component members return to find they have been moved to positions that are unequal to those they would otherwise have held had they not served in the military. Reserve component members also return home to positions that pay less and experience a lag in or loss of promotion because of their extended periods away from their civilian career.[5] These difficulties challenge both employers and employees who serve in the military as each tries to meet their obligations.

Reserve Component Members Face Unique Education-Related Challenges and Needs During Transition

We found that reserve component members attending higher education may enter and exit their schooling multiple times depending on the number of their deployments. Consequently, reserve component members face unique education-related challenges. First, reserve component members often do not know of their deployments in advance, so they cannot plan for when they will separate from school, how long they will be away, and when they will return. This prevents reserve component members from being able to plan for their educational progression.[6] Second, reserve component members encounter additional issues when they return from their deployments. Research indicates that they lag in coursework compared with their peers and may end up spending more time in college because of their military service.[7] Reserve component members are often older than their contemporaries, especially those who must leave school multiple times, which can lead to different relationships with

---

[4] Since the Civil Rights Division of the U.S. Department of Justice assumed USERRA enforcement authority in 2004 and through the end of fiscal year 2021, it has filed 113 USERRA lawsuits and favorably resolved 210 USERRA complaints (Office of the Assistant Secretary for Veterans' Employment and Training, *Uniformed Services Employment and Reemployment Rights Act of 1994: FY 2021 Annual Report to Congress*, U.S. Department of Labor, August 2022, p. 9).

[5] Bradford Booth, Mady Wechsler Segal, D. Bruce Bell, with James A. Martin, Morton G. Ender, David E. Rohall, and John Nelson, *What We Know About Army Families: 2007 Update*, Caliber, 2007, pp. 62–63; Michael E. Doyle and Kris A. Peterson, "Re-Entry and Reintegration: Returning Home After Combat," *Psychiatric Quarterly*, Vol. 76, No. 4, Winter 2005, p. 367; Jeffrey F Scherrer, Greg Widner, Manan Shroff, Monica Matthieu, Sundari Balan, Carissa van den Berk-Clark, and Rumi Kato Price, "Assessment of a Postdeployment Yellow Ribbon Reintegration Program for National Guard Members and Supporters," *Military Medicine*, Vol. 179, No. 11, November 2014, p. 1391; Laura Werber, Agnes Gereben Schaefer, Karen Chan Osilla, Elizabeth Wilke, Anny Wong, Joshua Breslau, and Karin E. Kitchens, *Support for the 21st Century Reserve Force: Insights on Facilitating Successful Reintegration for Citizen Warriors and Their Families*, RAND Corporation, RR-206-OSD, 2013, pp. 63–65; Sherrie L. Wilcox, Hyunsung Oh, Sarah A. Redmond, Joseph Chicas, Anthony M. Hassan, Pey-Jiuan Lee, and Kathleen Ell, "A Scope of the Problem: Post-Deployment Reintegration Challenges in a National Guard Unit," *Work*, Vol. 50, No. 1, 2015, p. 74.

[6] Mark Bauman, "The Mobilization and Return of Undergraduate Students Serving in the National Guard and Reserves," *New Directions for Student Services*, Vol. 126, Summer 2009, p. 15.

[7] Corey B. Rumann and Florence A. Hamrick, "Student Veterans in Transition: Re-Enrolling After War Zone Deployments," *Journal of Higher Education*, Vol. 81, No. 4, July/August 2010, pp. 444–445.

their fellow classmates.[8] Unfortunately for many reserve component members heading back to college, their schools often do not provide specific guidance or programming to address their particular needs. Consequently, many reserve component members must identify such processes and procedures themselves without formal institutional assistance.[9]

Reserve Component Members Face Unique Health-Related Challenges During Transition

We found that reserve component members may contend with specific health-related transition concerns. Because of the nature of their service, reserve component members must navigate multiple health care plans between the military and their civilian employers. This includes not only converting from military to civilian plans but also between military plans. Without careful management, this constant state of flux can result in gaps in health care coverage for service members and their families. Relatedly, reserve component members may not be able to find local health care providers that accept the military's health plans, especially if they live farther from highly populated areas and military installations.[10]

In addition, reserve component members may struggle with many of the same physical and mental health challenges as do active component veterans (e.g., injuries, depression, and posttraumatic stress disorder)—sometimes at higher rates than those in the active component.[11] Reserve component members may contend with friends and families who may not understand their deployment experiences, and without local military colleagues to turn to,

---

[8] Bauman, 2009, p. 21; Rumann and Hamrick, 2010, p. 442.

[9] Bauman, 2009, pp. 20–21.

[10] Institute of Medicine, Committee on the Initial Assessment of Readjustment Needs of Military Personnel, Veterans, and Their Families, *Returning Home from Iraq and Afghanistan: Preliminary Assessment of Readjustment Needs of Veterans, Service Members, and Their Families*, National Academies Press, 2010, p. 33; Werber et al., 2013, pp. 60–62.

[11] James Griffith, "Homecoming of Citizen Soldiers: Postdeployment Problems and Service Use Among Army National Guard Soldiers," *Community Mental Health Journal*, Vol. 53, No. 7, October 2017, p. 766; Lyndon A. Riviere, Athena Kendall-Robbins, Dennis McGurk, Carl A. Castro, and Charles W. Hoge, "Coming Home May Hurt: Risk Factors for Mental Ill Health in US Reservists After Deployment in Iraq," *British Journal of Psychiatry*, Vol. 198, No. 2, February 2011, p. 136; Nina A. Sayer, Kathleen F. Carlson, and Patricia A. Frazie, "Reintegration Challenges in U.S. Service Members and Veterans Following Combat Deployment," *Social Issues and Policy Review*, Vol. 8, No. 1, January 2014, p. 38; Scherrer, 2014, p. 1391; Wilcox, 2015, pp. 74–75.

this can lead to increased levels of emotional isolation.[12] Research shows that reserve component members desire more time than they receive to readjust to their civilian lives.[13]

Reserve Component Members Face Unique Financial Challenges During Transition

Reserve component members may also encounter specific financial issues spurred by their deployment cycles. Reserve component members must manage their financial commitments while shifting back and forth between different military and civilian salaries and schedules. To exacerbate these issues, reserve component members also have reported specific military pay issues and travel reimbursement delays.[14]

Reserve Component Members Face Unique TAP-Related Challenges

The literature highlights two major challenges that reserve component members have taking TAP: (1) the location and timing of taking TAP, and (2) scheduling and completing TAP within the allotted time. We discuss these challenges below.

Challenges with Where and When Reserve Component Members Take TAP

First, reserve component members may face difficulties with the geographical location of their TAP experience. Many reserve component members demobilize at active component installations far from their place of residence and work.[15] Consequently, they may not receive local guidance in terms of job seeking, house hunting, and cost of living.[16] The dislocation experienced by reserve component members in a demobilization site far from home might also cause feelings of isolation post-transition if they do not have local, direct access to assistance.[17] Reserve component members might also be distracted during their demobilization and unable to focus on their transition needs while preoccupied with returning home.[18]

---

[12] Doyle, 2005, p. 367; John F. Greden, Marcia Valenstein, Jane Spinner, Adrian Blow, Lisa A. Gorman, Gregory W. Dalack, Sheila Marcus, and Michelle Kees, "Buddy-to-Buddy, a Citizen-Soldier Peer Support Program to Counteract Stigma, PTSD, Depression, and Suicide," *Annals of the New York Academy of Sciences*, Vol. 1208, October 2010, p. 91.

[13] Bonnie M. Vest, "Reintegrating National Guard Soldiers After Deployment: Implications and Considerations," *Military Behavioral Health*, Vol. 2, No. 2, 2014, p. 228.

[14] Werber et al., 2013, p. 69.

[15] Booth et al., 2007, p. 63; U.S. House of Representatives, 2012b, p. 49; Agnes Gereben Schaefer, Neil Brian Carey, Lindsay Daugherty, Ian P. Cook, and Spencer R. Case, *Review of the Provision of Job Placement Assistance and Related Employment Services to Members of the Reserve Components*, RAND Corporation, RR-1188-OSD, 2015, pp. 2, 45; GAO, 2005, p. 22; GAO, 2014a, p. 26.

[16] U.S. House of Representatives, 2012b, p. 49; Schaefer et al., 2015, pp. 2, 45.

[17] Booth et al., 2007, p. 63; Werber et al., 2013, pp. 76, 79.

[18] GAO, 2005, p. 22; GAO, 2014a, p. 26.

We also found that because reserve component members are more likely to live farther from military stations and have less time to demobilize than active component members, reserve component members are more likely to elect to take the online version of TAP than the in-person course to fulfill their requirement. However, because "classroom instruction is the preferred method of instruction"[19]—the online version does not include the same level of personal interaction and guidance—some reserve component members may not receive the full benefits of TAP courses. In a 2021 report, GAO also found that some small or remote installations faced challenges in implementing TAP. For instance, some remote installations have few local employment opportunities for service members after they separate from the military.[20]

Challenges Scheduling and Completing TAP Within Allotted Time

Second, reserve component members may face additional challenges scheduling and completing TAP on time. Per TAP requirements, service members are meant to complete their TAP curriculum within the 90 days leading up to their separation.[21] Demobilization process times, however, vary widely between active duty and reserve component members. Active component members typically have 3–24 months to demobilize from duty. Reserve component members must demobilize within weeks. Despite this shortened timeline, reserve component members often do not receive additional active-duty time to ensure their full TAP participation. Finally, reserve component members often encounter conflicting commitments during their demobilization periods between mission requirements, commander demands, and transition components. Without commander support for their participation in TAP, reserve component members may feel that they cannot attend TAP courses.[22]

Findings from Our Discussions with Non-TAP Transition Service Providers

Although DoD provides transition resources and training to reserve component members through TAP, TAP is not the exclusive source for providing such resources to transitioning reserve component members. Veteran- and military-serving organizations at the national, state, and local levels also provide services to transitioning service members, including those in the Reserve Component. We conducted informational discussions with six nongovernmental service providers to gain insight on the transition needs of reserve component members. Participating providers represent the following organizations:

---

[19] GAO, 2014a, p. 15.

[20] GAO, 2021.

[21] DoD Instruction 1332.35, 2019, p. 39.

[22] GAO, 2005, pp. 22–24; GAO, 2014a, p. 27.

- Corporate America Supports You (CASY)
- Hire Heroes USA
- Illinois Joining Forces (IJF)
- Institute for Veterans and Military Families (IVMF) at Syracuse University
- Iraq and Afghanistan Veterans of America (IAVA)
- United Service Organizations (USO) Pathfinder.

Our discussion participants' extensive experience with and knowledge of reserve component members' needs provided complementary insights to those of military and other TAP stakeholders. We coded and analyzed our discussion data to identify: (1) transition needs specific to reserve component members, (2) recommendations to improve TAP programming, and (3) lessons learned from their experiences serving reserve component members. Our discussion protocol can be found in Appendix A.

During our discussions with non-TAP transition service providers, we asked whether they had observed common transition needs among reserve component members. Drawing on their responses, we identified needs in three areas: education, employment, and health. Many of these findings mirror findings from our literature review.

Education-Related Transition Needs

Regarding educational transition needs, three considerations arose. First, the service providers noted that reserve component members need assistance in better understanding the details of the GI Bill. This includes a clearer understanding of who is eligible to use the benefit (the reserve component member, their family members, etc.), and which specific benefits the law provides.[23] Second, interviewees stated that reserve component members could benefit from more awareness and knowledge of relevant educational certification opportunities because these could be particularly helpful in translating skills developed during military service. Interviewees also noted that reserve component members should receive guidance on how certification programs differ from more traditional educational paths and how to decide which option would best suit their particular needs.[24] Third, service providers stated that members should be instructed on how to identify educational institutions with connections to and an understanding of the U.S. military. They provided examples, such as schools that have military student organizations or have staff familiar with the U.S. military's education-related benefit programs like the GI Bill. Service providers also said it would be helpful to share information on which schools are designated as Yellow Ribbon schools (i.e., partici-

---

[23] Service providers from CASY, Hire Heroes USA, and IAVA, informational discussions with the authors, December 2017.

[24] Service providers from CASY, Hire Heroes USA, and USO Pathfinder, informational discussions with the authors, December 2017.

pants in the VA's Yellow Ribbon Program) and what types of additional support such schools provide to students.[25]

Employment-Related Transition Needs

In terms of employment-related needs, service providers' insights focused on military experience and employer relations. First, our discussion participants stated that reserve component members need to learn how to express the value of their military service throughout the employment application process. For instance, reserve component members need to know how to speak about their experience in interviews and create resumes that reflect both military and civilian experiences. Relatedly, our discussion participants highlighted that reserve component members need to learn and become aware of how they might apply the skills that they developed in the military to positions outside the military. They recommended doing so through educational coursework, professional certifications, and rotations in different military positions. Our discussion participants emphasized that reserve component members should start to think about the application of their skills outside the military well before they begin their transition, so they have time to take advantage of such opportunities.[26]

Second, service providers highlighted the need for more information-sharing regarding the potential challenges that reserve component members may face with employment because of deployments. Training and information on the protections that reserve component members have under USERRA are of utmost importance given the possibility of multiple deployments—in other words, multiple leaves of absence—from their civilian jobs. Discussion participants noted the additional concern of unemployment because of the strains that deployment places upon finding and keeping a job.[27] Related, one participant pointed out that many employers lack knowledge of and education on reserve component members' commitments and the legal protections provided to service members under USERRA.[28]

Health-Related Transition Needs

Finally, providers identified a few health-related needs unique to reserve component members.[29] One participant highlighted that some reserve component members live in rural areas

---

[25] Service providers from CASY and IVMF, informational discussions with the authors, December 2017. The Yellow Ribbon Program can help service members pay for higher out-of-state, private school, foreign school, or graduate school tuition and fees that the Post-9/11 GI Bill does not cover.

[26] Service providers from CASY, Hire Heroes USA, and USO Pathfinder, informational discussions with the authors, December 2017.

[27] Service providers from IAVA and IJF, informational discussions with the authors, December 2017 and January 2018.

[28] Service providers from IAVA, informational discussion with the authors, December 2017.

[29] Although we heard about health and health care–related needs enough times to warrant inclusion in these findings, these needs were mentioned less frequently than those related to education and employment.

where health care is sparse or few health care providers accept TRICARE, the U.S. military's health insurance. This could become a transition challenge if a reserve component member needs health care following a prolonged period of active duty.[30] Another service provider noted that reserve component members often lack knowledge about the health care benefits for which they are eligible or how to access them properly.[31] Yet another service provider observed that some reserve component members face similar mental health challenges after deployments or prolonged periods of active duty as active component members.[32] As mentioned earlier, it can be challenging for reserve component members to identify and access health care benefits to get the care that they need.

Recommendations for TAP Improvements

Because many non-TAP service providers either interact with TAP providers or work with individuals who have taken TAP, we asked interviewees about TAP and whether they had any recommendations to improve it. Drawing from their responses, we identified four areas for consideration: (1) TAP could better address reserve component members' transition needs, (2) TAP instructors should have military experience, (3) the timing of TAP should be shifted; and (4) TAP should be more flexible and customizable for reserve component members. We discuss these recommendations in more detail below.

TAP Could Better Address Reserve Component Members' Transition Needs

Service providers noted that TAP course content could be better suited to address reserve component members' needs. Multiple providers stated that the coursework should supply tailored assistance to individual members or to the Reserve Component specifically because the current version is too general and, consequently, unhelpful to reserve component members. Participants recommended that TAP not have a "one size fits all" approach.[33] One interviewee suggested that employment-focused information should not be too general or basic because that is not suitable for reserve component members who often are already employed or have worked extensively outside the military.[34]

Consequently, we included examples mentioned by only one discussion participant rather than requiring mention by multiple participants as we have done in the other two sections.

[30] Service providers from IVMF, informational discussion with the authors, December 2017.

[31] Service providers from IAVA, informational discussion with the authors, December 2017.

[32] Service providers from IAVA, informational discussion with the authors, December 2017.

[33] Service providers from Hire Heroes USA, IAVA, and IVMF, informational discussions with the authors, December 2017.

[34] Service providers from IJF, informational discussion with the authors, January 2018.

TAP Instructors Should Have Military Experience

Multiple non-TAP service providers recommended that TAP instructors be ex-military members because they have firsthand experience in transitioning from the military to civilian life and personally understand the process.[35] A couple interviewees suggested that instructors also should have complementary employment experience outside the military.[36] In other words, effective TAP instructors would be individuals who have successfully made the transition from the military to the civilian world. One provider also proposed that instructors be given more training in preparation for their position because, while they are often well-intentioned and supportive individuals, they do not receive the professional instruction and support that they need.[37]

The Timing of TAP Should Be Shifted

Service providers offered multiple suggestions regarding the timing of and time needed to complete TAP coursework. Multiple service providers indicated that reserve component members are not provided with enough time to complete TAP coursework. They recommended that reserve component members be given more time to complete their courses, so they can also take care of personal responsibilities and ensure that they are absorbing all the information provided in TAP classes.[38]

TAP Should Be More Flexible and Customizable for Reserve Component Members

Service providers made multiple recommendations about the need for more flexibility and customization of TAP for reserve component members. They also recommended that TAP be revised to address the specific needs of reserve component members. They see TAP programming as too broad, with more focus given to active component members' needs and considerations.[39] Another provider stated that the program should have more options to include local information. Because the program is administered across the country, much of the information provided is at a national level (which is not always directly applicable) rather than at the local level.[40] Relatedly, one participant proposed that more attention be provided at the

---

[35] Service providers from CASY, IAVA, and IVMF, informational discussions with the authors, December 2017.

[36] Service providers from CASY and IVMF, informational discussions with the authors, December 2017.

[37] Service providers from CASY, informational discussion with the authors, December 2017.

[38] Service providers from Hire Heroes USA, IJF, IVMF, and USO Pathfinder, informational discussions with the authors, December 2017 and January 2018.

[39] Service providers from CASY, Hire Heroes USA, and USO Pathfinder, informational discussions with the authors, December 2017.

[40] Service providers from IVMF, informational discussion with the authors, December 2017.

individual level while service members proceed through the TAP process.[41] Finally, several providers recommended increasing opportunities to connect TAP to community resources. They suggested that TAP administrators work more closely with local service providers, such as their organizations. One provider highlighted that government programs, including TAP, have such a broad mission that they could benefit from the resources that local providers offer. They proposed building more public-private partnerships as a mechanism to bring these resources together at both the local and national levels of the organizations.[42]

Lessons Learned from Non-TAP Transition Service Providers

During our informational discussions with non-TAP service providers, we inquired about any general lessons they had learned from supporting transitioning reserve component members. Two main themes emerged from their responses: (1) continued involvement post-transition and (2) programmatic flexibility. The service providers noted that the needs of reserve component members do not end once they have fully transitioned from the military to civilian world. The providers stressed the need for broadening the time horizon of support to post-transition veterans and establishing concrete processes for continued interaction. Such interactions could include matching veterans with service-providing organizations, which supply more long-term care and support.[43] Relatedly, our interviewees emphasized that programming for transitioning reserve component members should be as customized as possible. Transitioning reserve component members have unique experiences coming out of the military; thus, they require different types of support. The providers stressed that a one-size-fits-all-approach does not meet the unique needs of transitioning reserve component member populations.[44]

Insights on Managing the Transition Needs of Retiring Reserve Component Members

Although most transition support is focused on assisting service members who are separating from the military and reserve component members who are transitioning from extended active duty back to reserve duty, there is another population within the Reserve Component that also has unique transition needs: reserve component members who are transitioning into retirement and planning to permanently leave the military. We spoke with represen-

---

[41] Service providers from USO Pathfinder, informational discussion with the authors, December 2017.

[42] Service providers from CASY and IVMF, informational discussions with the authors, December 2017.

[43] Service providers from IAVA and IVMF, informational discussion with the authors, December 2017.

[44] Service providers from CASY and IVMF, informational discussion with the authors, December 2017.

tatives from the Air Force Reserve (AFR), Army National Guard (ARNG), and U.S. Coast Guard who are responsible for tracking retiring AFR, ARNG, and U.S. Coast Guard Reserve members to ask how they track reserve component members who are approaching retirement and whether they have identified any needs or considerations specific to this subpopulation of transitioning reserve component members.[45]

Processes for Managing Retiring Reserve Component Members

AFR and ARNG interviewees described how they manage reserve component members who are approaching retirement. What makes this subpopulation particularly challenging to manage is that many members of the Reserve Component may have a large gap or "gray area" of time (sometimes decades) from the time they last served on active or reserve duty and the time they are eligible for their military retirement benefits.[46] We spoke with each service's reserve administrators about how they attempt to maintain contact with retiring component members, especially when these members have not been on active or reserve duty orders for many years. According to AFR officials, AFR members are assigned a unit within the Air Reserve Personnel Center (ARPC). The ARPC tracks AFR members until they are four months out from reaching eligibility to start receiving their retirement pay and benefits, which occurs at 60 years old. At the four month–prior point, members receive a letter detailing the steps they need to take to prepare for receipt of their retirement pay. This process is standard across the Air Force, and outreach activities are handled at the unit level.[47]

For the ARNG, when an ARNG member approaches retirement, the responsibility for managing that member's account shifts from state-level Guard offices to the Army's Human Resources Command (HRC). HRC has been designated by the Army as the service's retirement lead for all members of the Army's Active, Reserve, and National Guard components. Consequently, state-level Guard units (the organizations that manage Guard members) are not able to track Guard members through their retirement process. This arrangement may create outreach difficulties because Guard members are accustomed to working with their state-level units. Our ARNG interviewees noted that some states still try to maintain contact with Guard members approaching and going through the retirement process. In these cases, Guard members may receive communications from their state-level units about retirement, even if they are not the official entity managing the retirement process.[48] ARNG officials also

---

[45] While the U.S. Coast Guard falls under the U.S. Department of Homeland Security and not DoD, Coast Guard members and reservists still take TAP. Thus, their inputs are relevant to the subject at hand.

[46] *Gray area retirees* are service members who have "served in the Guard or Reserve, are qualified for retired pay, and have retired from their service (stopped drilling), but are not yet at the age where they can start receiving retired pay. The time between their retirement from the service and the date when they are eligible to begin receiving retired pay [usually at 60 years old] is the 'gray area'" (Defense Finance and Accounting Service, "Gray Area Retirees," webpage, June 2, 2022).

[47] AFR officials, informational discussion with the authors, July 2018.

[48] ARNG officials, informational discussion with the authors, June 2018.

noted that the Army is developing a new integrated personnel and pay system, which would enable more communication and information-sharing for retiring Guard members between HRC and reserve component units.[49]

Key Considerations for Managing Retiring Reserve Component Member Transitions

Two key takeaways arose from our discussions with AFR and ARNG officials about keeping track of reserve component members as they approach retirement. First, reserve component members are not a captive audience leading up to their retirement as are active component members. The retiring reserve component subpopulation is more dispersed and less connected to their respective services, especially for those members for whom there is a gap in active service between meeting their 20-year service requirement and reaching retirement age. Officials described these gray area individuals as being in a "dead zone" in terms of regular communication and connection to their service. ARNG officials noted that they can lose track of these individuals once they are not participating in regular active service commitments. During this period, Guard members understandably focus on their civilian employment and lives outside the military, and thus, they may not maintain access to or knowledge of information needed for retirement pay and benefit issuance.[50]

Second, ARNG officials highlighted difficulties in managing retiring reserve component members because of challenges with limited support staff for keeping track of and issuing benefits to retiring reserve component members and shifting personnel systems. As noted earlier, in the ARNG, the responsibility for managing Guard members shifts from state-level units to the Army's HRC, making it much more difficult to keep track of retiring Guard members who are used to communicating and working with their respective home units. ARNG officials stated that the Army's HRC has traditionally focused on active component members because it manages their pay and benefits throughout their service careers.[51]

Interviewees recommended two strategies to address these issues. First, DoD could develop and incorporate a TAP course dedicated to the retirement process for reserve component members. This course would be taken as reserve component members reach their retirement eligibility age to help ensure they learn about the benefits for which they will be eligible. According to one official, it would be ideal to have someone develop and present

---

[49] We conducted our discussion with ARNG officials in summer 2018. Since then, the Army has rolled out some functionality of the Integrated Personnel and Pay System, beginning in 2020 with the National Guard and extending to the United States Army Reserve (USAR) and regular Army later in 2022. Two additional phases will follow, which include incorporating an additional 34 human resources and pay systems and the formation of a global payroll system. For more information, see U.S. Army, "IPPS-A: High Level Schedule," webpage, June 2021.

[50] ARNG officials, informational discussion with the authors, June 2018.

[51] ARNG officials, informational discussion with the authors, June 2018.

such a course who understands the specific needs of retiring reserve component members.[52] Second, interviewees emphasized the need for systems and processes that facilitate the collection of reserve component member information over time.[53] Having these in place would ensure that each of the services maintains current data for their reserve component members, so that retirement-related outreach is easier.

Combined Findings Regarding Reserve Component Transition Needs

Synthesizing our literature and informational discussion findings, we compiled a list of reserve component transition needs and challenges in seven key areas: (1) navigating employment challenges and accessing benefits, (2) navigating education-related challenges and accessing benefits, (3) navigating health care–related challenges and accessing benefits, (4) navigating financial challenges, (5) identifying and accessing retirement benefits, (6) accessing local transition services, and (7) navigating the timing of the TAP course. We discuss each of these key areas in the subsequent sections.

Transition Need: Assistance Navigating Employment Challenges and Accessing Benefits

Because reserve component members shift back and forth between military and civilian careers, they face unique employment difficulties as a result of multiple deployments. Our literature review and informational discussions highlighted three challenges for reserve component members: (1) job loss during or post-deployment (including USERRA violations and concerns), (2) unequal employment (including receiving lower-paying jobs after a deployment or experiencing a lag in or loss of promotion because of a deployment), and (3) work schedule inequities (e.g., loss of hours for hourly workers because an employer may perceive a reserve component member's absence as a lack of commitment toward their civilian job). Reserve component members need assistance navigating such challenges and accessing employment benefits for which they are eligible.

Transition Need: Assistance Navigating Education-Related Challenges and Accessing Benefits

Our findings indicate that deployment schedules place unique demands on reserve component members attempting to advance their education or training. In particular, the uncertainty surrounding the start date, return, and duration of deployments makes it difficult

---

[52] Coast Guard officials, informational discussion with the authors, June 2018.

[53] ARNG officials, informational discussion with the authors, June 2018.

to schedule near-term course schedules. The literature also indicates that reserve component members also face challenges upon their return from deployment. For instance, service members fall behind in coursework compared with their peers; their time spent in college is prolonged by deployments; there is an increased age discrepancy with fellow students on more-traditional paths, which may cause some service members to struggle to relate to their classmates; and service member integration processes are not established by many educational institutions. Findings from our informational discussions also indicate that transitioning reserve component members are frequently unsure about their GI Bill eligibility and may not pursue the full extent of opportunities available to them. Reserve component members need assistance navigating such challenges and accessing education-related benefits they are eligible for.

Transition Need: Assistance Navigating Health Care–Related Challenges and Accessing Benefits

Our literature review and informational discussion findings indicate that reserve component members have a host of transition challenges related to health care issues. For instance, some reserve component members live in geographically remote locations and have difficulty accessing physical and mental health care, and they must navigate multiple health care plans across the military, as well as juggling health care plans between the military and their civilian employer as they transition. Reserve component members need assistance navigating such challenges and accessing Reserve Component–specific health care benefits for which they are eligible.

Transition Need: Assistance Navigating Financial Challenges

Reserve component members face financial difficulties after deployments because of delays in military pay and travel reimbursements. Such delays are quite common among reserve component members as they move on and off active duty orders. These kinds of financial difficulties can compound and exacerbate stress, anxiety, and other mental health conditions. Reserve component members need assistance navigating such financial challenges—especially junior enlisted members who are more acutely affected by these types of challenges than transitioning reserve component members further along in their careers.

Transition Need: Assistance Identifying and Accessing Retirement Benefits

Our findings indicate that reserve component members have unique challenges as they approach the retirement eligibility age. Often, it is difficult for the services to maintain communication with reserve component members in the gray area—between the time a reserve component member last served on active or reserve duty and the time they become eligible for military retirement benefits. The greatest need among this subpopulation in the Reserve

Component is help identifying which retirement benefits a member is eligible for and how to access them.

TAP-Related Challenge: Geographical Access to Transitions Services

Geographic location can present several challenges during reserve component members' transitions. For instance, reserve component members may be geographically isolated from military installations, resulting in limited access to transition services both during and after their transition. Because reserve component members are also much more geographically distributed than active component members, commanders may have challenges communicating with reserve component members post-deployment. Guard members may also face more-acute challenges than reservists because Guard installations tend to be farther away from well-resourced, large active component installations that reservists can access regularly.

Geography can also cause challenges with taking TAP. For instance, because reserve component members often take TAP at demobilization sites (which are usually active component installations far from their homes), the TAP instructors do not have information that would enable them to refer reserve component members to transition resources in their state or local community. In addition, if reserve component members take TAP after they return to their homes from deployment, they may not be able to access as many transition resources because of their distance from active duty installations, and they may choose to take the online version of TAP, which may not provide them with the full benefits of the program.

TAP-Related Challenge: Timing of the TAP Course

Current TAP requirements provide reserve component members with only a few weeks to participate in TAP, compared with the several months that active component members have available to them. This brief availability window can create conflicting commitments between mission requirements, commander demands, and transition requirements. In addition, commander support for reserve component members' participation in TAP is sometimes lacking. As a result of these often conflicting demands, reserve component members may struggle to complete TAP while still on active duty.

Conclusion

The combined findings from our literature review and informational discussions served as the foundation for our understanding of reserve component transition needs. These findings also informed the questions that we developed for our focus group discussions with reserve component members in which we asked about their military-to-civilian transition needs and ways to improve transition support for them. In the next two chapters, we present our findings from these focus group discussions.

CHAPTER 4

Findings from Our Focus Groups: Transition Needs and Resources

To identify additional information about both the transition needs of reserve component members and the effectiveness of TAP in meeting those needs, we conducted focus group discussions with members from the reserve components. We convened a total of 31 focus groups with 153 reserve component members. Unfortunately, after multiple outreach attempts through multiple avenues, we were not able to include Air National Guard members or Marine Corps Reserve members, and we were only able to conduct one focus group with Army Reserve members. We began conducting our focus groups after receiving human subjects approval early in fall 2019. In March 2020, the onset of the coronavirus disease 2019 (COVID-19) pandemic caused us to pause and reevaluate our in-person focus group strategy because of the lockdowns and other public safety mandates that spread across the United States. We adopted an alternative strategy in which we conducted focus groups via telephone and teleconference via Microsoft Teams. During this time, it became clear how stretched the reserve components were as a result of their major role in the COVID-19 response across the United States, as well as other domestic missions, such as responding to protests during summer 2021 and the January 6, 2022, riot at the Capitol. Despite these unprecedented data collection challenges, we are confident in our focus group findings because we reached a point of *saturation* in our responses, meaning we repeatedly heard the same feedback and comments from our participants. That said, it is important to note that the findings from our focus groups were not derived from a representative sample of each of the service's reserve components, so this analysis does not include all perspectives from reserve component members.

Focus groups included both officers and enlisted personnel (usually in separate groups), and TAP participation varied among focus group participants. Participants were asked about their transition experiences, their transition needs, the quality and effectiveness of TAP in meeting those needs, and their perspectives on how TAP might be modified to better meet the transition needs of reserve component members. Our focus group protocols can be found in Appendix B. The total number of focus group participants, by officer or enlisted status and TAP participation, is presented in Table 4.1.

TABLE 4.1

Focus Group Participation by Reserve Component and TAP Experience

Service	Number of Focus Groups	Number of Officers Who Have Taken TAP	Number of Officers Who Have Not Taken TAP	Number of Enlisted Who Have Taken TAP	Number of Enlisted Who Have Not Taken TAP	Total Number of Participants
AFR	11	22	5	28	7	62
Army Reserve	1	4	0	4	0	8
ARNG	3	18	0	18	0	36
Navy Reserve	16	12	0	34	1	47
Total	31	56	5	84	8	153

During each focus group, two members of the research team were present—one led the focus group while the other took comprehensive notes. We then coded the notes from the 31 focus groups to systematically document participants' responses and identified five themes across participants' responses. The remainder of this chapter presents findings from our focus groups organized around two of these themes:

- reserve component members' perspectives on their transition experiences and needs
- reserve component members' perspectives on resources used during their transitions.

In Chapter 5, we present findings from our focus groups organized around the remaining three themes:

- reserve component members' positive experiences with TAP
- reserve component members' negative experiences with TAP
- recommendations from focus group participants on how to improve TAP and reserve component members' transitions.

Reserve Component Members' Perspectives on Their Transition Experiences and Needs

We began our focus groups by asking participants about their transition experiences and the kinds of needs they had during their transitions. Our analysis of the focus group data identified the following four areas of reserve component members' transition needs:

- employment
- health care
- finances
- education.

Of these, focus group participants expressed most concern about employment-, health care-, and finance-related transition needs.

Interestingly, our focus group findings overlap quite a bit with findings from our literature review and informational discussions (presented in Chapter 3). We discuss transition needs in each of these four areas in the subsequent sections with illustrative quotes from participating reserve component members.

Employment-Related Transition Needs

Employment-related transition issues are quite common among reserve component members as they go on and off orders and are deployed. Although many focus group participants mentioned that their employers were very supportive of their military service, others expressed that their relationships with their employers were more fraught because their employers were not supportive of their military service.

> Reservists [are] still looked at like the plague by employers; still that stigmatism of when she'll be gone for two weeks and what happens when she mobilizes; [that's] always in the back of employers' heads. (Navy Reserve focus group participant, enlisted)

> I've mobilized a couple of times and have had to get reintegrated with my employer. Reserve component members do not always have a great relationship with employers, so they need more help. (ARNG focus group participant, enlisted)

> When I first joined, my employer did not support me at all. It was a lot of "We're going to move you here, we're going to move you there" to accommodate their needs. At first I think they wanted to demote me and lower my pay. Then I found another employer who was very supportive of my Reserve service, but then I got a new supervisor and he put out a new job announcement for my position before I even went on orders. (AFR focus group participant, enlisted)

> My job hated that I left [on deployment]. Pretty much, they weren't going to promote me. Everyone had gotten promoted, but when it was time for my promotion, they hired two new hires and then I had to train them for the position I would have been promoted to. I worked for the government. My mission at work is to support the warfighter. They were acting like I did something wrong by deploying. When I extended my deployment, they were really [angry]. (Navy Reserve focus group participant, enlisted)

USERRA-Related Assistance

One of our most concerning findings is that reserve component members continue to experience USERRA violations, but they are unaware that their jobs are protected under USERRA. Both employers and reserve component members appear to need educating about the protections afforded to reserve component members under USERRA, while also increasing awareness among reserve component members on how they can contact the U.S. Department of Justice's Civil Rights Division if they run into an issue with their employers.

It would be helpful to have services out there to educate employers on USERRA when people cannot advocate for themselves in this way. (AFR force group participant, officer)

When I came off the initial accessions pipeline, I was essentially homeless and didn't have a job because my employer laid me off. I wasn't aware that USERRA protected our jobs. That was incredibly difficult—I came back to being a single parent and didn't have anything. No one told me to tell my [employer] that I'm protected under U.S. law. (Navy Reserve focus group participant, enlisted)

USERRA was one of our pre-deployment briefings. Someone was threatening to fire me, so I had the information to bring back to her. (AFR focus group participant, officer)

Unfortunately, we also heard of instances in which reserve component members did not have very supportive experiences when they reached out to the DOL's Veterans Employment and Training Service (DOL-VETS), for assistance:

Using USERRA was the most stressful thing I've ever done. I called [DOL-VETS] and thought that they would ask a set of questions and I would answer. I told her what was going on and she wasn't helpful. She sent me paperwork and told me my job was protected. USERRA was no help. Talking to [DOL-VETS] was more stressful than anything. . . . [The] aspect of TAP that was helpful was the info about USERRA/the [DOL-VETS] phone number. [DOL-VETS reps] need to be more caring on the other end [of the 1-800 number]. They need to ask more leading questions to help out. (AFR focus group participant, enlisted)

Assistance Finding a Job

Many of the reserve component members with whom we spoke (especially younger ones) indicated that finding and applying for a job was one of the main issues that they needed assistance with during their transition. This need included learning how to translate or match their military skills to the language used in civilian job descriptions, as well as learning how to find a job through employment sites, such as LinkedIn, Indeed, and Monster, and other more-specific job sites, such as USAJOBS. In addition, focus group participants indicated that transition support services that focus on resume writing were important to many of them because they had never had to write a resume.

Health Care–Related Transition Needs

Reserve component members would like more assistance in the area of health care–related transition issues. Many focus group participants indicated, in particular, that they needed help navigating the maze of issues that arose as they shifted across military health insurance plans and between military and civilian health insurance plans during their transition. This assistance includes providing more awareness and information to reserve component members regarding the Transitional Assistance Management Program (TAMP), which provides

180 days of health care benefits after regular TRICARE benefits end when reserve component members come off active duty orders.

> For me, I had some mental health stuff come [up] that had been present for a long time but came to a head [when I got home]. My particular medical department was like, here's all this stuff, you go figure it out. It takes a lot of time and coordination. It's easy to get lost in the shuffle. I ended up leaning on other service members and asking what had worked best for them. (Navy Reserve focus group participant, enlisted)

> I would like to see resources for dealing with loss, such as bereavement counseling. I wasn't dealing with it and hadn't faced it until I came back. (AFR focus group participant, enlisted)

> The insurance is always tricky when transitioning onto and off of orders—TRICARE, dental, etc. So that would be good knowledge to get help with. Being on long-term orders for a while and then having to transition back to the civilian world, it would have been helpful to get some preparation on how to speak the language in the civilian world. (AFR focus group participant, enlisted)

> I've heard different stories from other sailors on the confusion on what health benefits to apply for. (Navy Reserve focus group participant, enlisted)

> Reserve component members need more assistance with health care and TAMP. For instance, I took two TAP classes with TRICARE representatives, but nobody can answer my question about how to get reimbursed for wrong billing. (Navy Reserve focus group participant, enlisted)

> After I got off orders, no one explained to me how my health care works. I would unknowingly go without insurance for a month. Newer airmen just need that little bit of help regarding health care: TAMP, insurance, and medical. (AFR focus group participant, enlisted)

Finance-Related Transition Needs

Many focus group participants expressed that they needed assistance with financial issues during their transitions. The most prevalent financial concern among focus group participants was disruption in pay when they came off active duty orders: In some cases, reserve component members were not paid for four to five months after returning from deployment. Focus group participants indicated that TAP could provide important information about how to plan ahead should these pay issues arise.

> I would tell DoD and the Navy not to forget about me. I'm still waiting on pay issues from when I was mobilized. There's an attitude that we're not their concern anymore. We have a reserve [administrator] and they help. When I demobilized, they said they have to restart the process on the reserve side. I wish they'd taken care of it sooner. (Navy Reserve focus group participant, enlisted)

I have personally experienced this. I'm going to get paid, but it may not be until two months after later returning from deployment. If I was told this prior to deployment, I could have saved to have bills paid. It's a weird thing when you are kind of in between paychecks, counting on Navy pay but it didn't come through until two months later. I went to Fleet and Family Services, which was an amazing experience. I borrowed money easily and paid it back. (Navy Reserve focus group participant, enlisted)

Even when I did get paid, it wasn't correct until like month four or five after returning from deployment. A class or briefing that highlights military pay challenges would be very helpful. (Navy Reserve focus group participant, enlisted)

You need to go to the deployment readiness training. Put two months of income to the side because sometimes there are issues. What the Navy can do better is fix the pay system. A happy sailor is a paid sailor. Be financially prepared if their active duty accounts do not turn on at the time they're supposed to. I've seen some really bad situations. I've seen senior chiefs bring groceries to a family because they couldn't get their accounts turned on for over a month. (Navy Reserve focus group participant, enlisted)

I have three sailors in Afghanistan who have still not been paid. We're finding the right person to get their pay turned on. (Navy Reserve focus group participant, enlisted)

We have three groups of us on different deployments. All came back and all are having pay issues. We're working with the Marine Corps and Navy on administrative issues, but pay is constantly a problem. (Navy Reserve focus group participant, enlisted)

Education-Related Transition Needs

Reserve component members told us that they needed additional help with education-related transition needs. In particular, they indicated a need in identifying educational opportunities and navigating how to use their education-related benefits, especially their Post-9/11 GI Bill benefits.

I wish I had gotten more information from TAP on education. A lot of people are looking to go to school. I wasn't at that time, but if I had had the information, I may have been more interested in doing it. It's not always an easy thing, but having the right information, it would make it easier, especially if you had information about specific schools—e.g., here's who you can contact at this local school. (Navy Reserve focus group participant, enlisted)

We need mentorship to help you answer the important questions like: What do you need/ want? What education do you need? Can [the] GI Bill help you? (Navy Reserve focus group participant, enlisted)

TAP was helpful with GI Bill questions, but I had college plans squared away—[I] went right into the Reserve Component and college in hometown. (AFR focus group participant, enlisted)

Reserve Component Members' Perspectives on Resources Used During Their Transitions

During our focus group discussions, we asked reserve component members about the types of resources that they used during their transitions. We explored this issue because we wanted to get a sense of the breadth of resources that reserve component members use to address their transition needs. We found that reserve component members are using a wide variety of transition support services, but they mostly rely on DoD support programs and their colleagues. Some of the most common resources used by reserve component members are briefly discussed in the subsequent sections.

DoD Resources
Military OneSource
Military OneSource is a DoD-funded program that provides support resources related to various transition issues, such as tax services, spouse employment help, webinars and online training, relocation and deployment tools, childcare, elder care, and confidential nonmedical counseling services.[1]

TAP
As discussed in Chapter 2, TAP is a cooperative effort among DOL, DoD, the Departments of Education and Homeland Security, VA, SBA, and the Office of Personnel Management. TAP provides information and training to assist service members in making the transition from military to civilian life.[2]

Yellow Ribbon Reintegration Program
The Yellow Ribbon Reintegration Program (YRRP) is a DoD-wide effort to "promote the well-being of National Guard and Reserve members, their families and communities, by connecting them with resources throughout the deployment cycle." YRRP offers deployment support predeployment; during deployment; and 30, 60, and 90 days postdeployment.[3]

Service Resources
The services also offer many family support and family readiness services, including the Navy Fleet and Family Support Program, the Navy Expeditionary Combat Readiness Center, the Air Force Airman and Family Readiness Program, and the Army Soldier for Life Program.

---

[1] See Military OneSource, "About Us," webpage, undated.

[2] See DoD TAP, "Welcome to DoD TAP," webpage, undated-i.

[3] See YRRP, "About Us," webpage, undated.

Military Chain of Command

Focus group members indicated that they relied on their military chain of command as a resource for information on transitioning and lessons learned. In particular, focus group participants indicated that their immediate commanders were helpful in guiding them toward resources that aligned with their needs.

Unit Resources

We heard that, in some cases, reserve component members relied on unit resources, such as transition counselors and other support specialists, to help them navigate through challenges and access benefits.

State and Local Resources

Employment Centers

Focus group participants indicated that they connected with federal, state, and local employment centers, such as DOL's American Job Centers, or state and local employment centers. The overwhelming consensus among focus group participants was that these employment centers were far more helpful than most other employment resources because they had the best sense of the local job market and local employers.

Nongovernmental Resources

Hiring Our Heroes

Hiring Our Heroes is a nationwide effort led by the U.S. Chamber of Commerce Foundation to help transitioning service members and their spouses find employment by connecting service members with civilian employers.[4]

Veterans Service Organizations

Our focus group participants indicated that they reached out to veterans service organizations (VSOs) for various support services during their transitions, such as support in finding employment, but most of all, participants indicated that VSOs have been a valuable source of emotional support as they have navigated the transition process.

Other Resources

Colleagues

According to focus group participants, one of the most helpful transition resources are their fellow colleagues and friends who have already been through the process and are willing to

---

[4]   See U.S. Chamber of Commerce Foundation, "Hiring Our Heroes," webpage, undated.

share their lessons learned and experiences. This population can potentially be a force multiplier in helping reserve component members navigate their transitions.

Online Research

We learned that reserve component members conduct their own transition research online to supplement the information that they are receiving from other transition support resources. They indicated that online research is key to directly finding the resources that they need most.

CHAPTER 5

Findings from Our Focus Groups: Perspectives on TAP and How to Improve It

We asked focus group participants about their experiences with TAP—both positive and negative—so that we could better understand which aspects of TAP were helpful or unhelpful to reserve component members. Lastly, we asked our focus group participants for recommendations to improve TAP for reserve component members. This chapter discusses our findings on these three topics.

Reserve Component Members' Positive Experiences with TAP

When we asked about positive experiences with TAP, many focus group participants agreed that TAP is generally helpful—especially for young reserve component members, those who were returning from their first deployment or prolonged time on active duty, and those who wanted a refresher.

> Generally, TAP is informative and helpful in the content. Obviously, it's not useful for everyone all the time. But I found it helpful. By the third time, I didn't need anything except to just get back to school. (Navy Reserve focus group participant, officer)

> I was very impressed by first TAP class getting out of active duty/military; it was how I found a federal job. They had employers there to speak. I was scared as I didn't have anything set up. I wasn't expecting to get a job so soon. (Navy Reserve focus group participant, enlisted)

> When I took it in January, it was mostly reservists. We weren't being ignored. We got the information we needed. The health care situation is unique for reservists, but they covered that in the class. Didn't get the vibe that I was left behind because I was a reservist. (Navy Reserve focus group participant, officer)

Most Helpful Aspects of TAP

Focus group participants agreed that the most helpful aspects of TAP are the sections of the curriculum that focus on benefits. Although focus groups participants indicated that they wish TAP would focus more on Reserve Component–specific benefits, they still appreciated learning about the other benefits for which they are eligible.

> TAP was helpful; there are organizations that we might not know about, or we might know it exists but didn't know it was relevant. It was useful to have numbers for the VA, and I highlighted a lot of the materials. It was helpful to get that all at once. (AFR focus group participant, enlisted)

> TAP was very helpful—I didn't know to write a resume. Didn't need help finding job—had one lined up. Going into my most recent deployment, I had lessons learned from colleagues who had deployed. I heard who to talk to before deployment, etc. This made it easier to come home. (AFR focus group participant, enlisted)

Health Care–Related Portion of TAP Curriculum

Many focus group participants cited the VA benefits material in the TAP curriculum as being quite helpful. In particular, many participants thought that TAP provided valuable information regarding the complicated array of health care benefits—including disability benefits—provided by the VA.

> I did like the VA portion of the TAP course, the benefits available from that. But it sort of makes it seem like it's a simple application and then you'll be good to go. It's good knowledge to understand it's there, but as a reservist, I worry that a lot of folks might not do it because they don't want disability in case it affects their ability to be a reservist later on. And other reservists might not do it because it's not as easy as they make it seem, they might get discouraged. (AFR focus group participant, enlisted)

> The health care stuff was useful. (AFR focus group participant, enlisted)

> The VA benefits. I don't learn anything about the VA other than [through] TAP programs. (AFR focus group participant, officer)

> TAP helped teach us how to navigate the health system. The program gave really good information, especially the part of it on benefits, what you're entitled to, what to expect, who to contact if you have a question. Instructors gave out their phone numbers, emails, so we could start off there. (Navy Reserve focus group participant, enlisted)

> The most helpful part of TGPS [Transition Goals, Plan and Success component] was the afternoon we spent on VA benefits. (Navy Reserve focus group participant, officer)

> TAP was a long couple of days, but helpful. The portion regarding the VA and the VA documenting any service-connected issues or concerns you had. This was something I muddled through during prior deployments. (Navy Reserve focus group participant, enlisted)

Education-Related Portion of TAP

We heard from focus group members that the education-related portion of the TAP curriculum was helpful because many of them were planning to further their educations after returning from their prolonged time on active duty.

> TAP course offered a lot more information I didn't know; helped me in my reintegration into society. It really explained opportunities for some of us who didn't have a job or wanted to get a different career path. I was connected with a VA program, VET TEC Program, for going into IT positions, which I'm really trying to pursue now. (Navy Reserve focus group participant, enlisted)

Reserve Component Members' Negative Experiences with TAP

Focus group participants identified the following ten major concerns with TAP:

- Some commanders report that TAP requirements distract from military readiness.
- The 180-day active duty requirement results in having to take TAP multiple times with diminishing returns.
- TAP focuses on active component members' transition needs and does not adequately address reserve component members' transition needs.
- The information provided during TAP is not relevant to many reserve component members.
- The information in TAP is too broad and repetitive.
- TAP instructors and presenters are not familiar with reserve component members' transition challenges.
- Reserve component members feel like they get "dropped" or lost in the system.
- TAP does not connect service members to local transition resources.
- The timing and location of TAP are problematic for reserve component members.
- Reserve component members expressed frustration with the one-size-fits-all nature of TAP.

We discuss these concerns in detail with relevant quotes from focus group participants in the sections that follow.

Some Commanders Report That TAP Requirements Distract from Military Readiness

Some commanders participating in our focus group discussions expressed their frustration about TAP requirements distracting from military readiness. In particular, commanders stated that the timing of TAP distracts their service members from preparing for a deployment or carrying out a mission. For instance, several commanders indicated that the TAP requirement to begin planning for transition 365 days before a service member's transition has a direct impact on military readiness. Because of this requirement, commanders who are deploying for 365 days or more reported receiving pressure from TAP personnel to start their service members' transition planning *before* they had even left for deployment and right when commanders needed their service members to focus on the upcoming mission.

Although the 365-day requirement outlined in DoD Instruction 1332.35 may be appropriate for service members who are separating from the military, this requirement has very different consequences for reserve component members who must take TAP every time they are on active duty for more than 180 days.

> During deployment—by the nature of what we do—at any point, there are extremely busy periods. When you throw TAP in the mix, it adds stress, especially with no buy-in. We are only getting a few nuggets of info that are helpful in TAP. We need to focus on mission. (ARNG focus group participant, officer)

> TAP throws a wrench into the midst of training and everything else. You want to prevent burnout and stay physically/mentally fit before, during, and after deployment. Taking TAP adds to stress, especially when [it] has zero benefit to us. (ARNG focus group participant, officer)

> We are setting up to take TAP as soon as coming in on active duty. We should be focused on the mission and deploying, not focused on TAP. We are just checking the box so that TAP leaders will quit calling us. (ARNG focus group participant, officer)

> TAP is 16 hours of precious time that takes away from readiness. (AFR focus group participant, officer)

The 180-Day Active Duty Requirement Results in Having to Take TAP Multiple Times with Diminishing Returns

Many focus group participants had taken TAP many times during their careers—several as many as seven times because of the requirement to take TAP after being on active duty orders for 180 days or more. Some had even taken TAP multiple times within a short span of time, for example, twice in 18 months. Many focus group participants expressed frustration that they had to repeatedly take TAP and that each time they took it, it provided diminishing returns.

> I think TAP set me up pretty well as an E5 with resume writing, etc. As I've gotten more senior, it's less useful. I have a job. Last time, they asked what I wanted to get out of it. I want to know what has changed, anything new that is mandated, updates since the last time I took TAP. I was just trying to get back to my family. (Navy Reserve focus group participant, enlisted)

> You shouldn't have to take all of the classes over and over again. The classes don't matter and aren't relevant to the Reserve Component. At a certain point, it gets beyond ridiculous. (ARNG focus group participant, officer)

180 days makes no sense. I'm not transitioning. I do my reserve stuff, and then I go do my civilian stuff. (AFR focus group participant, officer)

What we hear from most of our people is that they are frustrated with the repetitiveness of program. (AFR focus group participant, officer)

Why do I have to keep doing this? We keep spinning our wheels. You should be able to provide proof that you've taken the classes before. (ARNG focus group participant, officer)

TAP Focuses on Active Component Members' Transition Needs and Does Not Adequately Address Reserve Component Members' Transition Needs

Many reserve component members stated that, in its current form, TAP does not address reserve component members' transition needs, such as those identified in Chapter 3. The current TAP curriculum does not consistently focus on identifying Reserve Component–specific employment, education, and health care benefits. Nor does it focus on issues such as strategies for planning or resolving disruptions in pay and benefits, which often occur when reserve component members come on and off active duty orders. In addition, the TAP curriculum does not focus on transition-related challenges that involve returning to a civilian employer or educational institution. For instance, our focus group participants indicated that there was not much information provided during TAP on employment protections provided by USERRA. Instead, TAP focuses on preparing active component members to separate from the military altogether and embark on a civilian career for the first time—a situation that is very different from a reserve component member who is not separating from the military but rather returning to an employer or school after their deployment.

The TAP classes are geared for [active component members] who do not have any form of [professional] experience. For those of us who sit through the TAP courses because we're unemployed only for the short-term or already have some employment already lined up, the TAP courses are useless. (ARNG focus group participant, enlisted)

Quite frankly, the way it's designed right now [TAP] doesn't fit reservist needs in my opinion. It's a very Active Component-centric program and needs to be shaped for reservists. Every time you come off orders as a reservist, you're asked to take TAP—even if you're coming off one set of active duty orders to another set of active duty orders, you're flagged to do TAP. (AFR focus group participant, officer)

As mobilized reservists, we are a foreign entity to active duty. If you are a reservist and you're mobilized, then pray that someone knows the reserve side. (Navy Reserve focus group participant, enlisted)

I didn't use any of the info I got out of TAP. If I'd been in a different stage of my career, it might have, but I didn't get any value. [Note: Participant was later in their career.] (Army Reserve focus group participant, officer)

The program touched briefly and vaguely about the transition process to get home to your family, but it was basically designed for a male combat arms guy with a stay-at-home wife. It was very glaring in the TAP stuff that it is designed for someone who joined the Army right after high school. Definitely not me. (Army Reserve focus group participant, officer)

They should make adjustments to the courses—especially regarding employment. Most of us [reserve component members] already have a job lined up or are going back to a job. (ARNG focus group participant, officer)

DoD needs to have the right people to take care of mobilized reservists for prior to deployment and for those when demobilizing. Currently, support staff is active duty and claim they don't know anything about the reserve side. (Navy Reserve focus group participant, enlisted)

The Information Provided During TAP Is Not Relevant to Many Reserve Component Members

As a consequence of TAP being focused on the transition needs of active component members, many focus group participants said that the information provided during TAP was not relevant to their situation or the unique transition challenges that reserve component members face as they switch between their military and civilian careers. For instance, most focus group participants expressed a desire for more information on Reserve Component–specific benefits, such as TAMP, as well as Reserve Component–specific processes, such as ensuring that their time on active duty is accurately accounted for (whether through a DD214 form or another way) to maximize their earned benefits while on active duty. Many focus group participants said that they would have liked to have received more-specific information on such things as the state of the local job market and local employers that are hiring from local support resources.

I did my first TAP course in the classroom and did the second one online. Honestly, they were both a waste of time. If I could have opted to not do it, I wouldn't have done it. I'm in the same unit, doing the same thing. (AFR focus group participant, enlisted)

Last April I was told that I couldn't go off orders and onto new orders until I sat through an active duty TAP course. I didn't need that; it was a "time waster" for me because I didn't need any of that stuff. The TAP coordinator understood my situation and tried to the best of her ability to shape the course to my needs. They let me skip the day on resume writing. If you're going to make it a requirement for me, then give me something I can use. In the end, I'd like to see a TAP program that addresses the true needs for a guardsman and reservist. Tell me what my benefits are [and] educate reservists on how long it takes to get your pay correct when transitioning on and off of active duty orders. (AFR focus group participant, officer)

The TAP courses overprepared me for things that I didn't need; they were treating me like I was a moron (telling me how to pay my bills and things like that). I'm an employment lawyer, I specialize in USERRA, and I couldn't figure out how to work the employment law part of it. So they were training me for things I didn't need, and I couldn't get training for the things I needed. They could have spent more time teaching us how to look for a postdeployment job while I was deployed and still active duty. (Army Reserve focus group participant, officer)

The overwhelming portion of the reserve component population doesn't need TAP. Only a small portion will benefit from taking it. (ARNG focus group participant, officer)

There might be some people who need [TAP], but for others, it's a horrible waste of time. (AFR focus group participant, enlisted)

The Employment Portion of TAP Is Particularly Irrelevant to Many Reserve Component Members

Focus group participants indicated that the employment portion of TAP is particularly irrelevant to many reserve component members because they already have civilian jobs and do not need help writing resumes or conducting a job search. Many focus group participants called for this portion of TAP to be changed to focus on issues more relevant to reserve component members' transitions, such as issues related to USERRA and how to navigate the challenges of repeatedly transitioning between military and civilian careers.

The majority of reserve component members have valid employment. TAP ought to be optional, not required. (ARNG focus group, participant, officer)

One thing that needs to be changed is the employment classes. For reserve component soldiers, 80 percent are already employed or have prior employment/experience with finding jobs and working in a workplace. (ARNG focus group participant, enlisted)

I had already been hired, so didn't need to job hunt. All the information was superfluous, and it was a pain in the butt. Dreading having to do it again. (AFR focus group participant, enlisted)

Majority of reserve component members have civilian occupation of some sort, so when they go through their transition, the courses are not applicable [because] they are returning to employment. (ARNG focus group participant, officer)

Second time around, [I] just flew through TAP because it was a mandatory requirement. I wasn't looking for a job. (AFR focus group participant, enlisted)

The least helpful part of TAP was the employment part. From the Reserve Component, we live this. This stuff is useless. (ARNG focus group participant, enlisted)

The Information in TAP Is Too Broad and Repetitive

Focus group participants expressed that the information in TAP is too broad for it to be helpful to reserve component members and that the course material is repetitive. Because TAP classes have very diverse groups of participants, which include service members across the components (and in some cases across services) and at various stages of their careers, much of the material addresses lowest common denominator issues. Most focus group participants told us that they were seeking more in-depth information on Reserve Component–specific issues, such as those mentioned in the previous sections.

> TAP does not really go in depth in terms of where to go for info. It shows you some options that are available, but not a lot of help to get you there. (Navy Reserve focus group participant, enlisted)

> The TAP content was very broad. For me, in my case, it wasn't relatable to me. (Navy Reserve focus group participant, enlisted)

> [When I took TAP], reservists were mixed in with active duty personnel who were leaving and some were going to the Reserve Component. It was very difficult with that combination of people. Trying to talk to both groups didn't work out well. (Navy Reserve focus group participant, enlisted)

> The repetitiveness of the program is the complaint we hear most from our people. (AFR focus group participant, officer)

> The information in TAP was provided in a generalized version, not the specifics as to how to do it—like how to check education eligibility. You miss the specifics in TAP. (Navy Reserve focus group participant, enlisted)

TAP Instructors and Presenters Are Not Familiar with Reserve Component Members' Transition Challenges

Many focus group participants indicated that most of their TAP instructors and presenters were unfamiliar with reserve component members' issues; therefore, the instructors were not able to answer their questions or direct them to appropriate transition support services. This concern seems to reinforce focus group participants' perspective that TAP information is not relevant to reserve component members.

> During workups [training periods] or demobilizations, [the instructors] are all active duty, and while they try to be helpful, we are a nuisance to them. (Navy Reserve focus group participant, enlisted)

> A lot of the instructors were active duty. They were still mentally out there. When active duty members are working with a reservist, you're a weekend warrior and such. Some things they said to us were upsetting. They don't know what we do on civilian side. (Navy Reserve focus group participant, enlisted)

> Active duty TAP presenters were giving incorrect information. They also sounded very hostile. I brought it up to the instructor. (Navy Reserve focus group participant, enlisted)

Reserve Component Members Feel Like They Get "Dropped" or Lost in the System

Many focus group participants told us that they feel frustrated and lost in a cookie-cutter bureaucratic system in which they do not know who to contact if they have questions about a transition-related issue. And if they can find a contact, they often get lost in the cold handoff from one provider to another. Therefore, many expressed the need to be able to talk one-on-one with someone, such as in a case management model in which a single point of contact can provide warm handoffs to other transition support providers to ensure continuity of support.

> I don't know who I call on base who's an expert if I run into an issue. Having a point of contact might be helpful. (AFR focus group participant, enlisted)

> In the Reserves, the hardest part is coming back and not having anyone to communicate with [about benefits]. (Navy Reserve focus group participant, enlisted)

> There is confusion. Who should I talk to? Who do I go to to get things signed? There's lots of uncertainty. (Navy Reserve focus group participant, enlisted)

> Someone needs to be identified as the follow-through organization/person. (Navy Reserve focus group participant, enlisted)

> I had a problem and spoke with people who gave the TAP course. No one was answering, and I was getting the runaround. It was like I needed to fly there and get the answers personally. Those contacts need to be available. They are supposed to deal with customer service. They need to have someone available to answer questions after TAP. You might have a question weeks after the course, but you can't ask them because they won't pick up the phone. (Navy Reserve focus group participant, enlisted)

> I initially left my civilian job and volunteered for a stateside mobilization. I didn't know I needed to do any transition program, I thought I'd just come off orders. There was nobody there to tell me that I had leave built up . . . to use. There's nobody in charge to tell you how to come off of orders. (Army Reserve focus group participant, enlisted)

> Sometimes we lose sailors because we just lose contact with them once they're off [active duty]. By the time you get in contact with them, you're limited in what you can do. For people who are transitioning all the way out, it's not a big issue, but if people want to continue into the reserves, there needs to be more effort made to make that handshake and get them transitioned. (Navy Reserve focus group participant, officer)

TAP Does Not Connect Service Members to Local Transition Resources

Prior RAND Corporation research on the *web of support* for reserve component members—the large constellation of non-DoD support resources available to reserve component members at the national, state, and local levels[1]—prompted us to ask whether TAP has connected reserve component members to local transition resources in their communities. Only a few reserve component members said that they had been connected to such resources. This lack of personal connection is a critical concern: Focus group participants overwhelmingly indicated that they want to connect with local resources rather than be directed to impersonal national resources or websites.

> Information in TAP is very national; they have no understanding of local sources. (AFR focus group participant, officer)

> We need to get resources for where we live, especially when we are not co-located [with a base]. Services should be offered closer to where you live, not just by/on base. (AFR focus group participant, enlisted)

> There were mentions of programs during TAP for my hometown, but they didn't elaborate on how to find those programs. I'm still unaware of where to find said programs. (Navy Reserve focus group participant, enlisted)

> It would probably be helpful for TAP to help connect us with these types of services, especially those located in the areas we are going to be living in. (Navy Reserve focus group participant, officer)

> I don't think generalized TAP in Norfolk should be the main TAP for the Navy. It should be held at NOSCs [Navy Operational Support Centers] where members are returning to get specialized information about what they need in their areas. (Navy Reserve focus group participant, enlisted)

The Timing and Location of TAP Are Problematic for Reserve Component Members

Focus group participants indicated that the timing of TAP (especially when it occurs at the end of a deployment) and the location of TAP (at a demobilization site) are problematic for reserve component members. Many focus group participants told us about instances in which reserve component members are taking TAP while they are demobilizing at an active component installation at the end of their deployment; reserve component members are not able to focus fully on TAP because they want to get back to their families. Therefore, some perceive TAP as an obstacle to being reunited with their families.

TAP Timing

> TAP has good topics. The program isn't trash, but the timing and repetitive nature [are] just not helpful. (AFR focus group participant, enlisted)

---

[1] Werber et al., 2013.

TAP should have been done before we deployed because when we get back in country, our whole focus is getting back to home, seeing family, getting business/work back together. Focus at that point is not the best, [we] don't want to sit anywhere longer than [we] have to. Between Norfolk and Camp Lejeune was about a week long; [I] started [TAP] as soon as I got back, but my attention span was about zero at that point. (Navy Reserve focus group participant, enlisted)

At the demobilization site, as senior leaders, we're taking a sigh of relief, so we're worn out—and want to get home to see our family. We don't want to rewrite a resume; we want to go home. The timing for TAP is way off to be beneficial. (ARNG focus group participant, officer)

Maybe we should have the option to take leave to go home and then come back to take TAP. That might make it more enticing. (Navy Reserve focus group participant, enlisted)

Biggest issue with timing: you're coming home and wanting to get home. Your mind is focused on getting home, even as they're giving resources to you. (Navy Reserve focus group participant, enlisted)

TAP Location

Right now, we rush through at demobilization but don't get the time to really use the program. (ARNG focus group participant, officer)

When you're coming back from a dangerous location, the last thing you want to be doing is staying longer than needed at a demobilization station. (Army Reserve focus group participant, officer)

Reserve Component Members Expressed Frustration with the One-Size-Fits-All Nature of TAP

Many focus group participants (especially more senior enlisted and officer reserve component members and those who have taken TAP repeatedly, despite not finding anything of value in portions of it) expressed frustration that TAP has a one-size-fits-all approach that does not take into account individual reserve component members' transition needs and experiences.

TAP focuses on the lowest common denominator. A [lieutenant colonel] is getting the same experience in TAP as a three-year guy without an education getting out [of the military]. Do an intake form to tailor the classes to something [he] needs to take. You shouldn't have to do all five days of TAP. (AFR focus group participant, officer)

It's hard when you do the transition for the first time. In 2015, I went from [active duty] to the Reserve Component for the first time. TAP is a very one size doesn't fit all experience, but you have to teach to the lowest common denominator. For me, I already had a college degree and knew how to write a resume, so I twiddled my thumbs all week. (Navy Reserve focus group participant, officer)

Focus groups participants also expressed frustration because the TAP administrative system views any kind of transition (e.g., from one service to another, from active duty to reserve duty, and from the Active Component to the Reserve Component) as separating or terminating from the military. This is why reserve component members find themselves repeatedly taking TAP.

> I took TAP before coming to the Reserves because they see you as "terminating," even though [I was] just going from one service to another. The system is not smart enough to recognize that type of transition. (AFR focus group participant, enlisted)

Recommendations from Focus Group Participants on How to Improve TAP and Reserve Component Members' Transitions

In our focus group discussions, we asked reserve component members for their recommendations on how to improve TAP and reserve component members' transitions. In this section, we focus on reporting the recommendations that focus group participants offered rather than evaluating the costs and benefits associated with each. The following recommendations emerged as the most common:[2]

- change the automatic requirement to take TAP after 180 days of active service
- make TAP more customized and flexible
- allow reserve component members to opt out of some or all of TAP based on their needs and experience
- include Reserve Component–specific transition challenges in TAP curriculum
- consider developing a Reserve Component–focused TAP course
- hire instructors, presenters, and counselors who are familiar with reserve component issues
- hold TAP courses locally and allow more flexibility in the timing
- connect reserve component members to local resources
- make TAP material more accessible
- provide access to one-on-one transition counseling
- consider shifting responsibility for TAP to the state-level Guard units
- collect regular feedback on TAP so continuous improvements can be made
- consider adding a mentorship component to transition assistance
- engage commanders more in the transition process.

We discuss each of these recommendations with relevant quotes from reserve component members in the sections that follow.

---

[2] We coded individual recommendations from focus group participants, and by analyzing recommendations across all focus groups, we determined this list of most common recommendations.

Change the Automatic Requirement to Take TAP After 180 Days of Active Service

The requirement to take TAP after being on active duty for 180 days or more is the primary source of much of the frustration expressed by focus group participants. This requirement results in reserve component members taking TAP repeatedly. There was no agreement among focus group participants on what the new time frame should be, but they agreed that the time frame should be longer than 180 days.

> Change the 180-day requirement. It's a waste of time if you've already done [TAP] once. As a reference, I do survival training every four years, and that's something my life depends on. It seems extraneous to do TAP so often. (Navy Reserve focus group participant, officer)

> Just don't require TAP every time after 180 days on active duty. We're sending the equivalent of a 20-year experienced person to waste their time. There clearly needs to be a trigger, such as if you've done TAP in the last five years or something. But pick a longer arbitrary [period] of time than 180 days. (AFR focus group participant, officer)

Make TAP More Customizable and Flexible

Focus group participants strongly agreed that TAP should be made more customizable and flexible. They stressed that TAP is currently too cookie-cutter or one-size-fits-all in its approach and that by treating everyone the same, TAP ignores individual needs, skills, and levels of experience.

> Home in on what an individual needs, generate an interview to the right person. Set up a one-on-one discussion with a counselor to identify needs that TAP can address. If I'm on orders for 180 days, I don't need it. It's now just a waste of time. (AFR focus group participant, officer)

> [TAP] has gotten better over time. I just went through it last November. A lot of it was geared toward someone who was younger and may have joined right out of high school, [who] doesn't have civilian workforce experience. It's stuff that someone older might not need. It would be better to customize to the individual. (Navy Reserve focus group participant, enlisted)

> You should be able to customize the course. The information is good, but all of the courses should be electives. (ARNG focus group participant, officer)

> I feel like we should be able to pick and choose what services I might need. GI Bill, starting college. I didn't know which scholarships I could apply to for tuition assistance. So if there were a list of courses that I could take, I could pick and choose, or opt out and check in next time. (AFR focus group participant, enlisted)

> An O4 takes TAP with lower ranks, even though they've been in for 15 years, so they need different information than an E4/E5. They need to work at tailoring TAP to the individ-

ual. Obviously, you can't tailor to every person because that would require more money, but some tailoring. (Navy Reserve focus group participant, officer)

If you've already done TAP, doing it again [seems unnecessary]. You could offer a one-day refresher—basically offer options to the service member instead of a one-size-fits-all mandate. (Navy Reserve focus group participant, officer)

Allow Reserve Component Members to Opt Out of Some or All of TAP Based on Their Needs and Experience

Focus group participants strongly agreed that reserve component members should be allowed to opt out of some or all of TAP based on their needs and experience. This change would alleviate the frustration among reserve component members who are taking the same courses repeatedly, even though some of them are not relevant.

Making [TAP] optional is important. You'll have people who won't be able to deal with another requirement because they have to focus on their job and are spread thin. (Navy Reserve focus group participant, officer)

Being brutally honest, I disregarded a lot of [TAP] because I have a job and didn't need transition assistance. (AFR focus group participant, enlisted)

I already had a job and was on military leave. I hated the class. I had a job, why am I doing this? It was long. (AFR focus group participant, enlisted)

Include Reserve Component–Specific Transition Challenges in TAP Curriculum

To make TAP more responsive to reserve component members' transition needs, its curriculum should incorporate more Reserve Component–specific transition issues. Again, this would address reserve component members' frustrations that TAP does not focus on issues that are relevant to them.

For the Guard/Reserve, they should focus instead on what they mess up: pay and health care benefits that are never right, leave that doesn't get processed. TAP could focus on this during demobilization, so members are not fighting for six to eight months to get that stuff right. We are three months past our mobilization, and some of our soldiers don't have TAMP right. They have not been able to use the benefit, and it's going to expire in three to four months. (ARNG focus group participant, officer)

It would be helpful if TAP could have more detail regarding reserve component transition in health care after demobilization and how to use medical [and] dental insurance. (Army Reserve focus group participant, enlisted)

TAP needs to have discussions more like this [the RAND focus group] so you can be more aware of issues. We need ongoing support to help us navigate Reserve Component–specific transition issues rather than rely on active duty sponsors or on TAP. (Navy Reserve focus group participant, enlisted)

Consider Developing a Reserve Component–Focused TAP Course

One of the options that we were asked to explore in this study was establishing a separate TAP course geared toward reserve component members. Focus group participants strongly agreed that DoD should consider developing a Reserve Component–focused TAP course. They argued that there is need for a separate TAP course for reserve component members because of differences in needs across the active and reserve components.

> There is a need for reserve [component] course. Maybe even a course for reservists as they're retiring. They still need to know more information, e.g., what to expect after retirement, what can you do if something goes wrong. (Navy Reserve focus group participant, enlisted)

> One course for reservists and one course for active duty [personnel] would be better since it [current TAP] is not super helpful for reservists. (Navy Reserve focus group participant, enlisted)

> In a perfect world, you may need a TAP just for the Guard and Reserves [that] then can be tailored for the individual based on their individual requirements. The program somehow needs to be flexible. Key issues to cover in the TAP course for reservists: get on top of your pay and start looking at your benefits (medical and dental) sooner rather than later. (AFR force group participant, officer)

> There should be a Reserve Component–only TAP course. Differences [across components] are so significant. TAP is definitely not directed at reservists, so [taking TAP] was really only delaying our process for getting back home. It made us more frustrated/agitated. And it got a little hostile when talking about the civilian world [because we have civilian jobs]. (Navy Reserve focus group participant, enlisted)

Hire Instructors, Presenters, and Counselors Who Are Familiar with Reserve Component Issues

As we noted earlier, focus group participants expressed frustration that few TAP instructors, presenters, and counselors are familiar with reserve component members' transition challenges. According to some focus group participants, by hiring instructors, presenters, and counselors who are familiar with such challenges, TAP will not only build its credibility among reserve component members but also will become a more relevant and more valuable resource to reserve component members.

> I would like to see more Selected Reserve representation in TAP—someone who understands the lingo and transition problems and who could hear from reservists directly. (Navy Reserve focus group participant, enlisted)

> I took two TAP classes with a TRICARE representative. Nobody could answer my questions. Health care and TAMP-related issues are areas that TAP needs better coverage for reserve component members. (Navy Reserve focus group participant, enlisted)

Hold TAP Courses Locally and Allow More Flexibility in the Timing

We heard a very strong demand signal from reserve component members that they want to take TAP closer to home where instructors and counselors are familiar with local employers and support resources. Reserve component members face challenges when they must complete TAP at the end of their deployment while they are still on active duty orders. Focus group participants indicated that increasing flexibility regarding the timing of TAP will alleviate multiple causes of stress that are currently placed on reserve component members.

Considerations for Pursuing a Localized Approach

As with every policy change, there are pros and cons to pursuing a more localized approach to delivering transition assistance.

> I think TAP should be held in the area where you live/drill rather than centrally located. (Navy Reserve focus group participant, enlisted)

> It makes a world of difference to go through TAP where you can see your family every day. We want to get back home. (Navy Reserve focus group participant, officer)

> Upper echelon/leadership mandated that people attend TAP, but this is not popular with sailors: They want to see their families. (Navy Reserve focus group participant, enlisted)

> It's tough because I'm in a TAP class in Virginia and there are people from all over the country. There should be a more localized approach. If I'm going back to Spokane, Washington, I need resources for that locality. (Navy Reserve focus group participant, officer)

However, some focus group participants cautioned against pursuing a localized approach:

> Going back to more localized approach, it could be good. But adding any extra load to a NOSC or my squadron—it's not going to work. In principle, it sounds great, but the system right now isn't set up to work like that. (Navy Reserve focus group participant, officer)

> I think maybe pushing down the information to the units, but pushing TAP training that far down potentially has issues. Some reserve units are amazing, and some not so much. You'd have varying levels of experience for TAP. (Navy Reserve focus group participant, enlisted)

Allow More Flexibility in Timing for TAP

Although focus group participants did not agree on the best time to take TAP, they did agree that reserve component members should have more flexibility in when they take the course. Such a change would allow reserve component members and their families to decide the best timing for their circumstances.

> When is the best time for TAP? I have asked myself that; as you're turning the doorknob to deploy, it is not beneficial. (Navy Reserve focus group participant, enlisted)

Whenever you have a blanket requirement like this, every reservist and deployment are different. Having the flexibility to do this program at various times would be really beneficial. Have a window of time when deployed in-country and a window of time when you get home to complete it. (Army Reserve focus group participant, officer)

If you can do it in one to two days on a drill weekend, that would make it easier. Also, add some information that focuses on state benefits that are readily available to a unit and provide that knowledge directly to soldiers. (ARNG focus group participant, enlisted)

TAP should not be done at demobilization. It could be done in a drilling duty status after demobilization. I feel very strongly about this. That's probably the right answer, as opposed to keeping us at a mobilization station where we're hating life. (Army Reserve focus group participant, officer)

Connect Reserve Component Members to Local Resources

Our findings indicate that TAP mostly connects reserve component members to national resources. At the same time, we heard very strongly from reserve component members that they would like TAP to connect them to local transition resources in their communities that know the local area in which they live. In this case, there appears to be a mismatch between what reserve component members perceive as the most helpful resources for them and the types of resources to which TAP is connecting reserve component members.

It would be better to do the course when you're back in your original location. Went through TAP in Norfolk but I'm from California, so local resources weren't helpful. It would make a huge difference to do TAP when you get back to your original location. Would help to have list of local contacts and be able to go to them when you get back. Time zone differences also make it difficult to utilize contacts from TAP. (Navy Reserve focus group participant, enlisted)

Additional resources would be extremely helpful. That would be something for the one-on-one session. Tweak the conversation for resources specific to my area for GI Bill benefits, college resources, and health care. (Navy Reserve focus group participant, enlisted)

Make TAP Material More Accessible

Many focus group participants indicated that it would be helpful if TAP material were made more accessible. They told us that there were times when they could not access the course materials because of barriers in accessing the information on government computers. In addition, focus group participants suggested that it would be very helpful to be able to access the course information after they have completed TAP when they have a question or need a refresher. Many focus group participants said that once they completed TAP, they could no longer access the course material. They also suggested making updates to policies, benefits, and other materials available online, enabling reserve component members to stay on top of such changes over time.

You need to be able to access the information worldwide, not just in [the United States]. Have it online. We had issues with being in EUCOM [U.S. European Command] and couldn't access info at Fort Bliss. (ARNG focus group participant, officer)

It's not like they can't make it available and let people review the information. It would be easy to say, if you want to review your benefits/other information, here's where you can go do that. (Navy Reserve focus group participant, officer)

Needs to be public facing—access anywhere and at any time—not just on a DoD machine. (ARNG focus group participant, officer)

Should have TAP slides online so service members can review it. This information should stay updated and include new information. As a supervisor, I would be able to find information and relay it. (AFR focus group participant, officer)

Almost every NOSC has a SharePoint page. Have those resources available there. Or have a TAP folder on the homepage. This would allow it to be customized: if you're in California, you need different information. You could have it on the Reserves homeport but then also on NOSC SharePoint for local resources. (Navy Reserve focus group participant, officer)

When you have TAP, there's a facilitator. They have all these people come in from outside agencies. All of the info (PowerPoints, handouts) can be made available. Once you've been through TAP, you have a good understanding of the landscape and know who to reach out to. If things have changed, you still generally know where to go and who can answer your questions. You can go through the material on your own initiative. (Navy Reserve focus group participant, officer)

Provide Access to One-on-One Transition Counseling

Many focus group participants never had the opportunity to meet with a TAP counselor; they expressed the need for personal, one-on-one counseling as reserve component members make their way through their transitions. This need to talk regularly with a counselor instead of consulting websites or other impersonal national transition resources was a dominant theme in our focus group discussions. Such one-on-one counseling could also potentially minimize reserve component members' stress and mental health issues during the transition process.

Should meet with a counselor so they can personalize/understand your situation. (AFR focus group participant, officer)

You should be able to talk with a personal counselor. (ARNG focus group participant, officer)

You should be required to talk with a counselor during TAP. (ARNG focus group participant, officer)

Should [assign] a counselor to each individual soldier—when you've been back for two weeks, then get call to help with resume, rather than being rushed through process at demobilization site. (ARNG focus group participant, officer)

A more tailored approach would be nice. A one-on-one appointment with a counselor would have helped; they could ask what you're worried about and what you need. I would prefer a one-on-one counseling session, not just "here are the resources." (Navy Reserve focus group participant, officer)

Sitting down with someone and going through what you need personally is more helpful than TAP. (AFR focus group participant, enlisted)

Consider Shifting Responsibility for TAP to the States for Guard Members

Many Guard members proposed that because the current version of TAP is so Active Component–centric and their transition needs were not being fully addressed, TAP for Guard members should be administered through the states. They argued that states are most familiar with the benefits that their Guard members are eligible for and this change would put transition resources closer to transitioning Guard members.

TAP should be funded by states. Have the course happen back at [a reservist's home] state rather than a demobilization site. Those at the state level have a better sense of what's in the state resources-wise. Not sure why the program is not a part of the local/state resources. Why can't we get everything done in one place? The state knows who the major employers are, who's veteran friendly, who's not—they don't know this at a faraway demobilization site. (ARNG focus group participant, officer)

Make TAP funded at the state. I care about my soldiers; the person at the demobilization site doesn't. (ARNG focus group participant, officer)

Collect Regular Feedback on TAP So Continuous Improvements Can Be Made

When we asked focus group participants if they had had an opportunity to provide feedback on TAP when they took the courses, a surprisingly large number told us that the RAND focus group was the first time they had such an opportunity. Although TAP instructors are supposed to provide TAP participants with a survey to fill out at the end of TAP, findings from our focus group discussions suggest that those surveys are not being administered consistently. Without this feedback, it is difficult to identify whether TAP is successfully and effectively addressing the transition needs of active and reserve component members and where there may be opportunities to improve TAP. Regular feedback would enable continuous improvements to be made to the program.

I was [able to provide feedback], but it might have been due to my rank. The instructor understood that the course didn't really meet my needs; I was lucky because she spoke a little bit of "reserve." If I'd been with a counselor who only understood the active duty portion of it, I could not have gotten that kind of feedback. I'm always amazed that we constantly talk about being a Total Force and the regular Air Force [doesn't] understand the Reserves at all. They just don't. If we could give reservists the chance to shape the course, that would be helpful. (AFR focus group participant, officer)

I just finished my sixth deployment. [This is the] first time anytime anyone has asked about my feelings on TAP other than a quick sheet at the end of the courses; I appreciate the chance to give this feedback. (ARNG focus group participant, officer)

I think this focus group is the first time I've gotten to give any official feedback on the TAP process. (Army Reserve focus group participant, officer)

I had to go run around between the online portion and the career counselor on the base, and they just apologized to me the whole time about how bad the program is. This is the first time I've been given a chance to provide feedback on it, which is probably why I've been so vocal. (Army Reserve focus group participant, officer)

The RAND study has been the only chance to provide feedback [on TAP] thus far. (AFR focus group participant, officer)

Consider Adding a Mentorship Component to Transition Assistance

Our focus group discussions surfaced a strong demand to establish a mentorship component to transition assistance. Focus group participants had various ideas on where mentors should reside (e.g., in TAP, at the unit level, or somewhere else), but the demand for this type of mentorship aligns with the need that they expressed for more one-on-one, personalized counseling during transition periods. Such mentors could also serve as additional sources of support for reserve component members—especially for those who cannot access other support services and, in turn, face isolation or other risk factors for mental health issues and suicide.

[We] need people who can serve as mentors [to transitioning reserve component members]. I would love to be that for someone since I've gone through this so much. (Navy Reserve focus group participant, enlisted)

[We need] someone in the unit or active duty side/reserve center as mentor through the process, [I] reach out to my sailors to check in on them regularly. [I] was assigned a person to check in on me/family, [but] no one ever did. Whatever that program was, that failed completely. [I] believe if the unit doesn't reach out, then the reserve center does not. (Navy Reserve focus group participant, enlisted)

Engage Commanders More in the Transition Process

Several commanders among our focus groups participants told us that they thought commanders should be more engaged in their service members' transitions because they have the best sense of their service members' needs and who in their units need to take TAP. By not engaging commanders in the transition process, TAP overlooks a key transition resource for reserve component members—especially those that do not have access to other transition support resources.

In menu of options, let the leaders lead, and if they send us a menu of things we can do, we can pick out what soldiers need—will do career track for those who are young and starting out. For those who are established, we can do courses on retirement or transitioning to the next step in their careers. We can tailor to the needs of our force (since we know those needs for each unit). (ARNG focus group participant, officer)

They should rely on leader engagement too—everyone (every leader) knows who in their unit needs TAP. A handful need it to help them better their civilian employment. You can encourage that better, but to require someone who's a teacher with a master's [degree] and an A-4 to do better by taking TAP, they don't need to do that. They need it [TAP] to be voluntary. (ARNG focus group participant, officer)

CHAPTER 6

Key Findings and Recommendations

Key Findings

The following key findings emerged from our analysis conducted through targeted literature reviews, informational discussions with transition assistance providers, and focus groups with reserve component members:

- Reserve component members have transition needs in seven key areas.
- TAP focuses on active component members' transition needs and does not adequately address reserve component members' transition needs.
- The 180-day active duty requirement results in reserve component members taking TAP multiple times with diminishing returns.
- The timing and location of TAP are problematic for reserve component members.

It is important to highlight that directly prior to publication of this report, the RAND study team learned through discussions with defense officials that DoD has already begun to address many of the recommendations, leveraging the authorities provided through the FY 2019 NDAA and resulting DoD-wide policies that came into effect while this study was underway. The services are providing increased one-on-one counseling and, in some cases, waiving attendance for reserve members who have recently completed the program after a 180-day deployment. Reserve component members, including many of the participants who expressed concerns, will feel the results of these efforts after future deployments. The results of the services' recent efforts are still being assessed.

We discuss key findings in more detail below.

Reserve Component Members Have Transition Needs and Challenges in Seven Key Areas

We found strong overlap among our findings that reserve component members have transition needs and challenges in seven key areas: (1) navigating employment challenges and accessing benefits, (2) navigating education-related challenges and accessing benefits, (3) navigating health care–related challenges and accessing benefits, (4) navigating financial challenges, (5) identifying and accessing retirement benefits, (6) accessing local transition services, and (7) navigating the timing of the TAP course. This finding provides critical insight into the unique transition needs of reserve component members and the areas in which DoD can focus its efforts to assist transitioning reserve component members.

TAP Focuses on Active Component Members' Transition Needs and Does Not Adequately Address Reserve Component Members' Transition Needs

We found that many reserve component members feel that, in its current form, TAP does not adequately address their transition needs. Instead, TAP focuses primarily on active component members who are preparing to separate from the military and embark on a civilian career for the first time. Many reserve component members (especially more-seasoned members) find that the material presented during TAP is not relevant to reserve component members and does not address the unique transition challenges that they face as they switch between their military and civilian careers.

Our analysis also found that many TAP instructors, presenters, and counselors were not familiar with reserve component issues; therefore, they were not able to answer Reserve Component–specific questions or direct reserve component members to the appropriate transition support services and, in some cases, provided incorrect information related to reserve component policies. Such problems seemed to reinforce reserve component members' perspective that reserve component issues are secondary in TAP and that some of the information presented during TAP is irrelevant to reserve component members.

The 180-Day Active Duty Requirement Results in Reserve Component Members Taking TAP Multiple Times with Diminishing Returns

We found that many focus group participants had taken TAP several times during their careers—some as many as seven times—because of the requirement to take TAP after being on active duty orders for 180 days or more. Some had even taken TAP multiple times within a short span of time, for example, twice in 18 months. Many of our focus group participants expressed frustration that they had to repeatedly take TAP and that each time they took it, it had diminishing returns. This issue is the root of other reserve component members' concerns related to TAP, such as TAP is repetitive, TAP is a one-size-fits-all model and is too rigid, and more-senior service members who have attended TAP previously should be able to opt out of parts or all of TAP.

Timing and Location of TAP Are Problematic for Reserve Component Members

We found that the timing (especially when TAP is at the end of a deployment) and the location of TAP (especially at a demobilization site) are problematic for reserve component members. Many focus group participants told us that when reserve component members are taking TAP while they are demobilizing at an active component installation at the end of their deployment, they are not fully focused on TAP because they want to get back to their families. Therefore, some reserve component members perceive TAP as an obstacle to being reunited with their families after a deployment.

Recommendations

Drawing on our key findings, we offer the following recommendations for improving TAP to better address the transition needs of reserve component members:

- change the automatic requirement to take TAP after 180 days of active service
- make TAP more customizable and flexible to meet individual transition needs
- ensure reserve component members have access to one-on-one counseling
- consider developing a Reserve Component–focused TAP course
- connect reserve component members to the broader web of state and local transition resources through TAP
- collect regular feedback on TAP so continuous improvements can be made to the program
- increase synergies between TAP and YRRP
- provide more transition assistance to retiring reserve component members.

We discuss these recommendations in more detail in the sections that follow.

Change the Automatic Requirement to Take TAP After 180 Days of Active Service

The current requirement that mandates reserve component members to take TAP every time they are on active duty for 180 days or more is a major source of frustration because it leads them to taking TAP multiple times over a short period of time. Even if reserve component members have taken TAP multiple times or are simply returning to their previous job, they are still required to take the same courses and receive the same information as first-time TAP participants. Focus group participants' opinions differed on what the revised required time frame for taking TAP should be; however, they agreed that it should be longer than 180 days. Focus group participants also agreed that TAP is quite helpful for junior enlisted members and those returning from deployment for the first time.

We recommend that the 180-day requirement for reserve component members to take TAP be revised. Because this requirement was mandated by the *VOW to Hire Heroes Act* of 2011, Congress will likely need to make any changes to it. An alternative requirement that might better meet the needs of reserve component members is to require all reserve component members returning from their first time on active duty orders of 180 days or more to take TAP but then allow them to opt in to take sections of TAP in the future as their careers progress and needs dictate. A requirement for all reserve component members to take a short refresher TAP course every five years or so may also be helpful to ensure that reserve component members keep up to date on changes in benefits for which they are eligible.

Make TAP More Customizable and Flexible to Meet Individual Transition Needs

Our discussions with reserve component members highlighted their strong wish for TAP to be more customizable and flexible in order to meet individual members' transition needs. Reserve component members are frustrated by TAP's current one-size-fits-all model, which ignores reserve component members' needs, skills, and experience. We recommend that DoD consider enabling reserve component members to tailor their TAP experience by allowing them to opt into courses and receive information that they need most, while opting out of courses and information that they do not need at various points in the progression of their military and civilian careers.

Ensure Reserve Component Members Have Access to One-on-One Counseling

As stated earlier, many focus group participants had never had a one-on-one session with a counselor. Because the 2019 TAP changes emphasized the importance of one-on-one counseling and because our findings show high demand for such counseling, we recommend that DoD ensures that TAP offers an option for one-on-one counseling to reserve component members. This will likely require additional DoD resources within the services or in other DoD support resources, such as Military OneSource. Our discussions with reserve component members highlighted the need for a more high-touch, personalized approach to transition assistance. Reserve component members want to talk with human beings, rather than collect information online or consult impersonal, national support resources. A one-on-one counseling option could also identify early any challenges that individuals face and provide them with necessary resources. It would also address reserve component members' concern that they currently "get lost in the system" and do not know how to access benefits.

Consider Developing a Reserve Component–Focused TAP Course

One of the options that DoD asked us to explore in our study is whether there is a need to establish a separate TAP course for reserve component members. Our findings compel us to recommend that DoD consider developing such a Reserve Component–focused TAP course. Significant differences in transition needs between active and reserve component members warrant separate courses. We recommend that this course focus on issues that typically challenge reserve component members after returning from prolonged active duty, such as issues related to pay, access to health care and other support services, and health insurance and other benefits. Such a course could also greatly increase TAP's effectiveness in addressing the transition needs of reserve component members. If the development of a separate Reserve Component–specific course is found to be unfeasible because of funding or other reasons, we recommend that DoD add at least one component to the current TAP curriculum that focuses on reserve component transition challenges and needs.

Connect Reserve Component Members to the Broader Web of State and Local Transition Resources Through TAP

During our focus groups, reserve component members said that they would like to access transition resources closer to the communities in which they live for greater ease of access; however, we also heard that very few TAP participants had been connected to state and local resources through TAP or their service. RAND's previous work on reintegration support for Guard and Reserve families identified a broader web of support for reserve component members and their families.[1] This web of support consists of various support resources, including government organizations; private nonprofit organizations; private-for-profit organizations; faith-based organizations; and informal resources, such as family, friends, and social networks.[2] We recommend that DoD help link transitioning reserve component members to this broader web of support resources in a manner similar to other initiatives to support service members and military families, such as Joining Forces and the Military Spouse Employment Partnership, to enable reserve component members to access state and local resources closer to home.[3] DoD does not need to "do it all," but by connecting reserve component members to this broader network of support, DoD could expand its efforts to help transitioning reserve component members and provide them with services closer to home. Success in linking to this wider web of resources will require DoD to allocate the necessary personnel and resources to get a picture of the organizations postured to support transitioning reserve component members and create a means, such as a website, to facilitate connections.

---

[1] Werber et al., 2013.

[2] Werber et al., 2013, p. 84.

[3] Joining Forces is a White House–led initiative that involves coordination and intensive communication among government and nongovernmental organizations (White House, "Joining Forces," webpage, undated). The Military Spouse Employment Partnership establishes an informal roster of companies that seeks to employ military spouses (DoD, "Military Spouse Employment Partnership," webpage, undated).

Collect Regular Feedback on TAP So Continuous Improvements Can Be Made to the Program

When we asked focus group members whether they had had an opportunity to provide feedback on TAP after taking the course, a surprisingly large number told us that the RAND focus group was the first time they had had such an opportunity. Although TAP instructors are supposed to provide TAP participants with a survey to evaluate their TAP experience, our focus group findings suggest that those surveys are not being administered consistently. Therefore, we recommend that surveys and other opportunities to provide feedback on TAP be administered consistently. Without this feedback, it is difficult to identify the extent to which TAP is effectively addressing the transition needs of active and reserve component members and opportunities for improving TAP.

Increase Synergies Between TAP and the Yellow Ribbon Reintegration Program

DoD's YRRP was established in the National Defense Authorization Act for Fiscal Year 2008.[4] It is a legislatively mandated program intended

> to support the Services in providing National Guard and Reserve members and their families with critical support, information, services, and referrals throughout the entire deployment cycle (pre, during and post) to maximize successful transitions as Service members move between their military and civilian roles and to create strong, resilient military families.[5]

Accordingly, YRRP events are held at various points throughout the deployment cycle: predeployment, during deployment, 30 days after demobilization, 60 days after demobilization, and 90 days after demobilization. However, implementation of YRRP varies across services and units (e.g., in some services, attendance is mandatory at all YRRP events; in others, attendance is voluntary). In most cases, YRRP events last one to two days and feature a series of speakers who focus on specific topics related to the deployment cycle (e.g., employment, mental health).

Because YRRP focuses on providing support to reserve component members during the entire deployment cycle, increasing synergies between TAP and YRRP would benefit transitioning reserve component members. For instance, TAP could draw from YRRP instructors who are familiar with common reserve component challenges associated with returning from deployments or prolonged time on active duty orders. In addition, TAP and YRRP

---

[4] Public Law 110-181, National Defense Authorization Act for Fiscal Year 2008, Sec. 582, Yellow Ribbon Reintegration Program, January 28, 2008.

[5] YRRP, *Fiscal Year 2011: Annual Report to Congress*, Office of the Assistant Secretary of Defense for Reserve Affairs, March 2012, p. 2.

should leverage each other's network of providers to broaden the pool of support services to which reserve component members have access.

Provide More Transition Assistance to Retiring Reserve Component Members

Unlike active component members who are retiring, retiring reserve component members face myriad challenges, including a gap, or gray area, between the time a reserve component member last served on active or reserve duty and the time they are eligible for their military retirement benefits. This gap can often be decades long, which leads to challenges in keeping track of reserve component members nearing retirement age and in ensuring that they understand their retirement benefits and know how to collect them. Our findings indicate that this unique subpopulation within the Reserve Component needs more transition support. The main question is how will the services keep track of and continue to support retiring reserve component members both when they separate from the military and when they approach retirement eligibility. According to those we spoke with in the course of this study, TAP and other transition support providers could serve as important resources for this subpopulation by distributing updated information on retirement benefits and the process for collecting them. This information could be provided through a refresher TAP course that reserve component members could take when they become eligible for retirement benefits.

Concluding Thoughts

Although TAP is DoD's largest transition support resource for both active and reserve component members, our research findings have begun to identify areas in which TAP is not effectively addressing reserve component members' transition needs. These findings present critical opportunities for improving reserve component members' transition experiences. We know that transitions can be a vulnerable period for some reserve component members as they adjust to myriad changes and potential stressors, which can lead to mental health issues and even suicide. The recommendations that we have outlined in this report offer a potential roadmap to DoD for improving TAP to better support reserve component members during transitions between their military and civilian lives.

Non-TAP Service Provider Discussion Protocol

Introduction

1. Can you please tell us your name, the name of your organization, and your position?
2. What are your organization's mission and goals?

Target Population

1. Can you please tell me which populations within the armed services your program targets?
2. Can you provide an estimate for the number of members served each year?
   a. Do you track participation by type of service member? If so, which categories do you include?
   b. [if they track Reserve and Guard members] Can you share data on the number of Reserve and Guard members you serve each year?
3. What marketing methods do you employ to reach your target population?

Program Implementation

1. What types of needs are addressed by your program?
2. What services or activities does your program provide to address each of these identified needs?
3. Does your program offer tailored modules, information, or services for specific subgroups within your service population?
   a. [if Reserve Component is not mentioned] Do you provide modules or services specifically for Reserve Component and National Guard members?
      i. If so, what kinds of services do you provide?
      ii. If not, are considerations for Reserve and Guard members already incorporated into your program, and if so, how?

Reserve Component Needs: General Considerations

1. Do you serve both active and Reserve/Guard members?
   a. If so, do you see any general differences between the two groups' transition experiences?
      i. If so, what are they?
2. What unique needs, if any, do you hear about or observe with Reserve and Guard members?
   a. [if they provide unique needs] How does your current programming address each of the identified needs?
   b. [if a unique need is not specifically addressed] How might your program be changed to better address this need?

Coordination with External Service Providers

1. Do you work directly with any local Transition Assistance Program (TAP) provided by each of the military services?
   a. If so, what methods of communication and coordination do you use?
   b. Are you aware of which of your services are requested most from TAP participants?
2. If you have worked with TAP directly, do you have any recommendations on how the program might improve its coordination and cooperation with external service providers?

Program Assessment

1. How do you measure the effectiveness of your program?
   a. How often do you conduct performance assessments?
2. Do you provide options for Reserve and Guard members to submit specific needs-based requests or recommendations?
   a. If so, what are those options?
3. What is your process for making changes based upon the feedback you receive?

Reserve Component Needs: Additional Issue Area Questions

Employment Considerations

Reserve and Guard members are often called into active duty multiple times and consequently may face difficulties with their employer when they return home.

1. Can you provide examples of unique employment-related needs that you have seen in your work with Reserve and Guard members?
2. Does your program address the specific needs of Reserve and Guard members regarding their civilian career development? If so, how?
   a. Are there specific services to help those who may have lost their job due to their periods of absence?

Health Care and Insurance Program Considerations

Reserve and Guard members transition back and forth between civilian and military health plans multiple times depending on their number of deployments.

1. Can you provide examples of health care- and insurance-related needs that you have seen in your work with Reserve and Guard members?
2. Do you provide guidance on how best to navigate health care coverage between on and off duty periods?
   a. Does your program provide information on how best to handle multiple transitions between TRICARE and employer-provided plans?

Education Considerations

Reserve and Guard members may enter and exit their institutions of higher education multiple times depending upon the number and length of their deployments, which can cause challenges for their progression to degree attainment.

1. Can you provide examples of education-related needs for Reserve and Guard members who may already be enrolled in college or might be in the future?
2. Do you partner or work with colleges and universities to help them understand the unique needs faced by their Reserve, Guard, and veteran students?

Focus Group Protocols

Protocol for Focus Groups with Reserve Component Members Who Have Taken TAP

Collect the following demographic data from each participant:

- In which service(s) and component (Reserve, National Guard) have you served?
- What is your total time in active and/or reserve military service?
- What is your rank and pay grade?
- How many times have you gone through the Transition Assistance Program (TAP) curriculum?
- Did you take TAP because you were demobilizing/deactivating following a minimum of 180 days of active duty?
  - If not, please specify your status that triggered the requirement to attend TAP (e.g., transitioning from active duty in the active component to the Reserves or National Guard, transitioning from a definite/indefinite recall, retiring from active duty).
  - Approximately how long ago did this happen?
- Did you take the online TAP, brick-and-mortar course, or a combination of both?
  - [for those who took online TAP] Why did you take the online version?

Section A: Questions Regarding Reserve Component Transition Experiences and Needs

We'll now talk about your transition experiences—particularly, we want you to focus on your ability to return to or find a job, return to your schooling, speak about your health concerns (including mental health concerns), your interactions with your family and friends, or your ability to reintegrate back into your community. (Note that if you have a mixture of transitions and separations, make sure that you clarify which experience you're describing.)

1. Were you prepared to make the transition from active duty or to leave the military?
   a. If so, what helped you be prepared?
   b. If not, what would have made you more prepared?

   i. [probes, if needed] Transition Goals, Plans, Success (GPS) curriculum;[1] returning to your employment or employer; returning to your schooling?

2. How many of you *returned* back to the job or education program you had before you were activated or mobilized or before you prepared to retire/separate from the military?

  a. How supportive was your employer of your continued service in the Guard or Reserve?

  b. Do you know what factors led your employer to hold this view?

3. How many of you were looking for a *new* job or education program when you transitioned from active duty, retired, or separated from the military?

4. What kinds of concerns, needs, or problems did you experience during your transition?

  a. [probes, if needed] Transition GPS curriculum?

  b. Returning to your employment or employer?

  c. Returning to your schooling?

  d. Seeking or receiving health care assistance (including for mental health concerns)?

  e. Reintegrating with family, friends, and community?

5. What transition support resources did you utilize during the transition process? These could include resources in your state or local community, other transitioning service members, veterans service organizations, and state or local employment agencies.

  a. Which of these support services were most effective and why?

  b. Which of these support services were least effective and why?

  c. Were there any support services that you were interested in but could not access? If so, why not?

  d. Did the TAP connect you to any of these other transition support services?

6. What would make transitions easier for Guard and Reserve members?

  a. What could DoD do?

  b. What could your service do?

7. What recommendations would you provide to other Guard and Reserve members who are about to make this transition?

Section B: Questions Regarding Reserve Component Experiences with TAP

1. Was there sufficient time for you to prepare to transition?

  a. How long before your transition from active duty or your separation date did you actually begin your pre-separation counseling?

---

[1] The TAP curriculum used to be known as "Transition GPS." In 2019, it became known simply as the TAP curriculum.

    b. How far into your transition did you take the Transition GPS curriculum?

2. Please provide your thoughts on the timing of when TAP is administered. For instance, TAP is currently administered while demobilizing/deactivating, while still on active duty, or retiring or separating from military service. Is this the best time during a Guard or Reserve member's career to receive this material?
    a. If not, is it too early or too late? How could the timing be improved for Guard and Reserve members?

3. Did you have enough time to complete TAP after returning from active duty?
    a. If not, why?

4. For those of you who do not live near an active duty base/installation, did you have any difficulty accessing *all* TAP transition support services (pre-separation counseling, the five-day core curriculum, two-day additional tracks, additional assistance with resume writing, additional financial counseling, Capstone, etc.)?

5. Think about your participation in TAP (such as the counselors, instructors, the location, the facilities, class content). Are there areas that could be improved for Guard and Reserve members?
    a. How could the training, services, and resources you received better address these concerns, needs, or problems?

6. Which parts of TAP were *most* helpful to you? Why?

7. Which parts of TAP were *least* helpful to you? Why?

8. Did you have any remaining transition-related concerns, questions, or needs after you took the TAP course?
    a. If so, what were they?

9. Were your active duty and Reserve/National Guard commanders supportive of you taking part in TAP and did they allow you the time necessary to complete all the components you *wanted* to attend, not just those you were *required* to attend?
    a. If not, why not?

10. When did you learn about the TAP's career readiness standards (CRS)?
    a. Was this too early, too late, or just about at the right time in your career?
    b. Did you have enough time—and the right resources—to prepare you to achieve the CRS?

11. For those of you who already had a job waiting for you, did the TAP materials help you learn how to get another job in the future?

12. If not, what would you have wanted to learn to help you get another job in the future?
    a. How many of you knew you could waive the employment module of TAP because you had a job waiting for you?
        i. How many times did you waive the employment module of TAP?

13. During the TAP process, were you given opportunities to provide feedback on how TAP could better meet your transition needs?

Protocol for Focus Groups with Reserve Component Members Who Have Not Taken TAP

Collect the following demographic data from each participant:

- In which service(s) and component (Reserves, National Guard) have you served?
- What is your total time in active and/or reserve military service?
- What is your rank and pay grade?
- Are you a full-time reserve component member?
- Are you a Traditional Reservist/Guardsman?
- How many times have you been on continuous active duty orders for at least 90 days?

We'll now talk about your transition experiences—particularly, we want you to focus on your ability to return to or find a job, return to your schooling, speak about your health concerns (including mental health concerns), your interactions with your family and friends, or your ability to reintegrate back into your community. (Note that if you have a mixture of transitions, separations, and departures to make sure that you clarify which experience you're describing.)

1. Were you prepared to make the transition from active duty or to leave the military?
    a. If so, what helped you be prepared?
    b. If not, what would have made you more prepared?
        i. [probes, if needed] Additional transition support, returning to your employment or employer, returning to your schooling?
2. How many of you *returned* back to the job or education program you had before you were activated or mobilized or before you prepared to retire/separate from the military?
    a. How supportive was your employer of your continued service in the Guard or Reserve?
    b. Do you know what factors led your employer to hold this view?
3. How many of you were looking for a *new* job or education program when you transitioned from active duty, retired, or separated from the military?
4. What kinds of concerns, needs, or problems did you experience during your transition?
    a. [probes, if needed] Lack of transition support?
    b. Returning to your employment or employer?
    c. Returning to your schooling?
    d. Seeking or receiving health care assistance (including mental health concerns)?
    e. Reintegrating with family, friends, and community?
5. When do you typically start planning for your transition/reintegration process?
    a. Have you used any resources to help you with that planning?

6. What transition support resources did you utilize during the transition process? These could include resources in your state or local community, other transitioning service members, veterans service organizations, and state or local employment agencies.
   a. Which of these support services were *most* helpful to you and why?
   b. Which of these support services were *least* helpful to you and why?
7. For those of you who live near an active duty base/installation, have you had any difficulty accessing transition/reintegration support services?
   a. If so, were you able to ultimately access these services and, if so, how?
8. For those of you who do not live near an active duty base/installation, have you had any difficulty accessing transition/reintegration support services?
   a. If not, how did you access these services?
   b. If so, were you able to ultimately access these services and, if so, how?
9. What do you think is the best time during a Guard or Reserve member's career to receive transition/reintegration support?
10. Did you have any remaining transition-related concerns, questions, or needs after your transition?
    a. If so, what were they?
11. Have your active duty and Reserve/National Guard commanders been supportive of you utilizing transition/reintegration support services?
    a. If not, why not?
12. What would make transitions easier for Guard and Reserve members?
    a. What could DoD do?
    b. What could your service do?
13. What recommendations would you provide to other Guard and Reserve members who are about to make this transition?

Abbreviations

AFR	Air Force Reserve
ARNG	Army National Guard
CASY	Corporate America Supports You
CRS	career readiness standards
DoD	U.S. Department of Defense
DOL	U.S. Department of Labor
FY	fiscal year
GAO	U.S. Government Accountability Office
GPS	goals, plans, success
HRC	Human Resources Command
IAVA	Iraq and Afghanistan Veterans of America
IJF	Illinois Joining Forces
ITP	individual transition plan
IVMF	Institute for Veterans and Military Families
MOU	memorandum of understanding
NDAA	National Defense Authorization Act
NOSC	Navy Operational Support Center
SBA	U.S. Small Business Administration
TAMP	Transitional Assistance Management Program
TAP	Transition Assistance Program
VA	U.S. Department of Veterans Affairs
USAR	United States Army Reserve
USERRA	Uniformed Services Employment and Reemployment Rights Act
USO	United Service Organizations
YRRP	Yellow Ribbon Reintegration Program

Bibliography

Ackerman, Robert, David DiRamio, and Regina L. Garza Mitchell, "Transitions: Combat Veterans as Students," *New Directions for Student Services*, Vol. 126, Summer 2009.

Aquino, Genedine Mangloña, *Texas National Guard and Reserve Members and Veterans: Post-Deployment and Reintegration Problems and the Services to Meet Those Needs*, Texas State University-San Marcos, 2013.

Bauman, Mark, "The Mobilization and Return of Undergraduate Students Serving in the National Guard and Reserves," *New Directions for Student Services*, Vol. 126, Summer 2009.

Booth, Bradford, Mady Wechsler Segal, D. Bruce Bell, with James A. Martin, Morton G. Ender, David E. Rohall, and John Nelson, *What We Know About Army Families: 2007 Update*, Caliber, 2007.

Castaneda, Laura Werber, Margaret C. Harrell, Danielle M. Varda, Kimberly Curry Hall, Megan K. Beckett, and Stefanie Stern, *Deployment Experiences of Guard and Reserve Families: Implications for Support and Retention*, RAND Corporation, MG-645-OSD, 2008. As of September 8, 2022:
https://www.rand.org/pubs/monographs/MG645.html

Center for the Study of Traumatic Stress, *Military Families in Transition: Stress, Resilience, and Well-Being Conference Report*, Department of Psychiatry, Uniformed Services University of the Health Sciences, 2014.

Code of Federal Regulations, Title 32, National Defense; Chapter I, Office of the Secretary of Defense; Subchapter D, Personnel, Military and Civilian; Part 88, Transition Assistance for Military Personnel; Section 88.2, Applicability and Scope.

Defense Finance and Accounting Service, "Gray Area Retirees," webpage, June 2, 2022. As of July 7, 2022:
https://www.dfas.mil/RetiredMilitary/plan/Gray-Area-Retirees/

Department of Defense Instruction 1332.35, *Transition Assistance Program (TAP) for Military Personnel*, U.S. Department of Defense, September 26, 2019.

DoD—*See* U.S. Department of Defense.

DoD Instruction—*See* Department of Defense Instruction.

DoD TAP—*See* DoD Transition Assistance Program.

DoD Transition Assistance Program, "About DoD TAP," webpage, undated-a. As of September 8, 2022:
https://www.dodtap.mil/dodtap/app/about/DoDTAP

DoD Transition Assistance Program, "Capstone," webpage, undated-b. As of September 8, 2022:
https://www.dodtap.mil/dodtap/app/transition/capstone

DoD Transition Assistance Program, "Career Readiness Standards (CRS)," webpage, undated-c. As of September 8, 2022:
https://www.dodtap.mil/dodtap/app/about/career_readiness_standards

DoD Transition Assistance Program, "Career Readiness Standards Overview," fact sheet, undated-d.

DoD Transition Assistance Program, "Initial and Pre-Separation Counseling," webpage, undated-e. As of September 8, 2022:
https://www.dodtap.mil/dodtap/app/transition/pre-seperation_counseling

DoD Transition Assistance Program, "Military Life Cycle (MLC) Model," webpage, undated-f. As of September 8, 2022:
https://www.dodtap.mil/dodtap/app/about/mlc

DoD Transition Assistance Program, "TAP Curriculum," webpage, undated-g. As of April 15, 2022:
https://www.dodtap.mil/dodtap/app/transition/core_curriculum

DoD Transition Assistance Program, "Two-Day Tracks," webpage, undated-h. As of April 15, 2022:
https://www.dodtap.mil/dodtap/app/transition/tracks

DoD Transition Assistance Program, "Welcome to DoD TAP," webpage, undated-i. As of September 8, 2022:
https://www.dodtap.mil/dodtap/app/home

DoD Transition Assistance Program, *Personal Financial Planning for Transition Participation Guide*, 2018.

DoD Transition Assistance Program, *Military Occupational Codes Crosswalk: Participant Guide*, U.S. Department of Defense, 2021.

Doyle, Michael E., and Kris A. Peterson, "Re-Entry and Reintegration: Returning Home After Combat," *Psychiatric Quarterly*, Vol. 76, No. 4, Winter 2005.

GAO—*See* U.S. Government Accountability Office.

Greden, John F., Marcia Valenstein, Jane Spinner, Adrian Blow, Lisa A. Gorman, Gregory W. Dalack, Sheila Marcus, and Michelle Kees, "Buddy-to-Buddy, a Citizen Soldier Peer Support Program to Counteract Stigma, PTSD, Depression, and Suicide," *Annals of the New York Academy of Sciences*, Vol. 1208, October 2010.

Griffith, James, "Decades of Transition for the US Reserves: Changing Demands on Reserve Identity and Mental Well-Being," *International Review of Psychiatry*, Vol. 23, No. 2, April 2011.

Griffith, James, "Homecoming of Citizen Soldiers: Postdeployment Problems and Service Use Among Army National Guard Soldiers," *Community Mental Health Journal*, Vol. 53, No. 7, October 2017.

Gross, Natalie, "TAP Is Getting a Makeover This Year. Here's What You Need to Know," *Military Times*, June 28, 2019.

Harvey, Samuel B., Stephani L. Hatch, Margaret Jones, Lisa Hull, Norman Jones, Neil Greenberg, Christopher Dandeker, Nicola T. Fear, and Simon Wessely, "Coming Home: Social Functioning and the Mental Health of UK Reservists on Return from Deployment to Iraq or Afghanistan," *Annals of Epidemiology*, Vol. 21, No. 9, September 2011.

Hotopf, Matthew, Lisa Hull, Nicola T. Fear, Tess Browne, Oded Horn, Amy Iversen, Margaret Jones, Dominic Murphy, Duncan Bland, Mark Earnshaw, et al., "The Health of UK Military Personnel Who Deployed to the 2003 Iraq War: A Cohort Study," *The Lancet*, Vol. 367, No. 9524, May 2006.

Institute of Medicine, Committee on the Assessment of Readjustment Needs of Military Personnel, Veterans, and Their Families, *Returning Home from Iraq and Afghanistan: Preliminary Assessment of Readjustment Needs of Veterans, Service Members, and Their Families*, National Academies Press, 2010.

Institute of Medicine, Committee on the Assessment of Readjustment Needs of Military Personnel, Veterans, and Their Families, *Returning Home from Iraq and Afghanistan Preliminary Assessment of Readjustment Needs of Veterans, Service Members, and Their Families*, Phase 2, National Academies Press, 2013.

Iversen, Amy C., and Neil Greenberg, "Mental Health of Regular and Reserve Military Veterans," *Advances in Psychiatric Treatment*, Vol. 15, No. 2, March 2009.

Maung, Joanna, Johanna E. Nilsson, LaVerne A. Berkel, and Patricia Kelly, "Women in the National Guard: Coping and Barriers to Care," *Journal of Counseling and Development*, Vol. 95, No. 1, January 2017.

Military OneSource, "About Us," webpage, undated. As of July 7, 2022:
https://www.militaryonesource.mil/about-us/#serve

Milliken, Charles S., Jennifer L. Auchterlonie, and Charles W. Hoge, "Longitudinal Assessment of Mental Health Problems Among Active and Reserve Component Soldiers Returning from the Iraq War," *JAMA*, Vol. 298, No. 18, November 2007.

Office of the Assistant Secretary for Veterans' Employment and Training, *Uniformed Services Employment and Reemployment Rights Act of 1994: FY 2021 Annual Report to Congress*, U.S. Department of Labor, August 2022.

Public Law 110-181, National Defense Authorization Act for Fiscal Year 2008, Sec. 582, Yellow Ribbon Reintegration Program, January 28, 2008.

Public Law 112-56, VOW to Hire Heroes Act, November 21, 2011.

Public Law 115-232, John S. McCain National Defense Authorization Act for Fiscal Year 2019; Section 552, Improvements to Transition Assistance Program, August 13, 2018.

Riviere, Lyndon A., Athena Kendall-Robbins, Dennis McGurk, Carl A. Castro, and Charles W. Hoge, "Coming Home May Hurt: Risk Factors for Mental Ill Health in US Reservists After Deployment in Iraq," *British Journal of Psychiatry*, Vol. 198, No. 2, February 2011.

Rumann, Corey B., and Florence A. Hamrick, "Student Veterans in Transition: Re-Enrolling After War Zone Deployments," *Journal of Higher Education*, Vol. 81, No. 4, July/August 2010.

Sayer, Nina A., Kathleen F. Carlson, and Patricia A. Frazier, "Reintegration Challenges in U.S. Service Members and Veterans Following Combat Deployment," *Social Issues and Policy Review*, Vol. 8, No. 1, January 2014.

Schaefer, Agnes Gereben, Neil Brian Carey, Lindsay Daugherty, Ian P. Cook, and Spencer R. Case, *Review of the Provision of Job Placement Assistance and Related Employment Services to Members of the Reserve Components*, RAND Corporation, RR-1188-OSD, 2015. As of September 8, 2022:
https://www.rand.org/pubs/research_reports/RR1188.html

Scherrer, Jeffrey F., Greg Widner, Manan Shroff, Monica Matthieu, Sundari Balan, Carissa van den Berk-Clark, and Rumi Kato Price, "Assessment of a Post-Deployment Yellow Ribbon Reintegration Program for National Guard Members and Supporters," *Military Medicine*, Vol. 179, No. 11, November 2014.

Shields, Duncan M., David Kuhl, Kevin Lutz, Jesse Frender, Niki Baumann, and Philip Lopresti, *Mental Health and Well-Being of Military Veterans During Military to Civilian Transition: Review and Analysis of the Recent Literature*, Canadian Institute for Military and Veteran Health Research and Scientific Authority, Veterans Affairs Canada, April, 11, 2016.

Thompson, Jim, Linda VanTil, Jill Sweet, Alain Poirier, Kristofer McKinnon, Sanela Dursun, Kerry Sudom, Mark Zamorski, Jitender Sareen, David Ross, Claudine Hoskins, and David Pedlar, *Canadian Armed Forces Veterans: Mental Health Findings from the 2013 Life After Service Survey*, Research Directorate, Veterans Affairs Canada, March 19, 2015.

U.S. Army, "IPPS-A: High Level Schedule," webpage, June 2021. As of July 7, 2022:
https://ipps-a.army.mil/high-level-schedule/

U.S. Chamber of Commerce Foundation, "Hiring Our Heroes," webpage, undated. As of July 7, 2022:
https://www.uschamberfoundation.org/hiring-our-heroes

U.S. Code, Title 10, Chapter 58, Benefits and Services for Members Being Separated or Recently Separated, Sections 1141–1153, January 3, 2012a.

U.S. Code, Title 10, Chapter 58, Section 1142, Preseparation Counseling; Transmittal of Certain Records to Department of Veterans Affairs, January 3, 2012b.

U.S. Department of Defense, "Military Spouse Employment Partnership," webpage, undated. As of February 20, 2023:
https://msepjobs.militaryonesource.mil/msep/

U.S. Department of Defense, "Interagency Statement of Intent Among the Department of Defense, Department of Veterans Affairs, Department of Labor, Department of Education, United States Office of Personnel Management, and United States Small Business Administration Regarding the Redesigned Transition Assistance Program for Separating Service Members," August 15, 2013.

U.S. Department of Defense, "Memorandum of Understanding Among the Department of Defense, Department of Veterans Affairs, Department of Labor, Department of Education, Department of Homeland Security (United States Coast Guard), United States Small Business Administration, United States Office of Personnel Management Regarding the Transition Assistance Program for Service Members," January 31, 2014.

U.S. Department of Defense, *Pre-Separation Counseling Resource Guide*, October 2021.

U.S. Department of Defense, *2022 TAP Curriculum: Financial Planning for Transition*, 2022a.

U.S. Department of Defense, "Transition Assistance Initial Self-Assessment Worksheet," 2022b.

U.S. Department of Justice, "Uniformed Services Employment and Reemployment Rights Act of 1994 (USERRA)," webpage, July 31, 2019. As of September 8, 2022:
https://www.justice.gov/servicemembers/
uniformed-services-employment-and-reemployment-rights-act-1994-userra

U.S. Department of Labor, *Department of Labor Employment Workshop (DOLEW): Participant Guide*, January 2021.

U.S. Department of Veterans Affairs, *VA Benefits and Services Participant Guide*, undated.

U.S. Government Accountability Office, *Military and Veterans' Benefits: Enhanced Services Could Improve Transition Assistance for Reserves and National Guard*, GAO-05-544, May 2005.

U.S. Government Accountability Office, *Transitioning Veterans: Improved Oversight Needed to Enhance Implementation of Transition Assistance Program*, GAO-14-144, March 2014a.

U.S. Government Accountability Office, *Veterans Affairs: Better Understanding Needed to Enhance Services to Veterans Readjusting to Civilian Life*, GAO-14-676, September 2014b.

U.S. Government Accountability Office, *Transitioning Veterans: DOD Needs to Improve Performance Reporting and Monitoring for the Transition Assistance Program*, GAO-18-23, November 2017.

U.S. Government Accountability Office, *Military Personnel: DOD's Transition Assistance Program at Small or Remote Installations*, GAO-21-104608, July 2021.

U.S. House of Representatives, *Oversight Plans for All House Committees*, 110th Congress–115th Congress, U.S. Government Publishing Office, 2007–2017.

U.S. House of Representatives, Back from the Battlefield: DOD and VA Collaboration to Assist Service Members Returning to Civilian Life: Joint Hearing Before the Committee on Armed Forces and Committee on Veterans' Affairs, U.S. Government Printing Office, July 25, 2012a.

U.S. House of Representatives, Examining the Re-Design of the Transition Assistance Program (TAP): Hearing Before the Subcommittee on Economic Opportunity of the Committee on Veterans' Affairs, U.S. Government Printing Office, September 20, 2012b.

U.S. House of Representatives, Lowering the Rate of Unemployment for the National Guard and Reserve: Are We Making Progress? Hearing Before the Subcommittee on Economic Opportunity of the Committee on Veterans' Affairs, U.S. Government Printing Office, March 14, 2013a.

U.S. House of Representatives, Status of Implementation of the Requirements of the VOW Act and the Recommendations of the Presidential Veterans Employment Initiative Task Force for the DoD Transition Assistance Program—Goals, Plans, and Success (GPS): Hearing Before the Subcommittee on Military Personnel of the Committee on Armed Services, U.S. Government Printing Office, April 24, 2013b.

U.S. House of Representatives, A Review of the Transition Assistance Program (TAP): Hearing Before the Subcommittee on Economic Opportunity of the Committee on Veterans' Affairs, U.S. Government Publishing Office, January 27, 2015a.

U.S. House of Representatives, Transition Assistance Program—A Unity of Effort: Hearing Before the Subcommittee on Military Personnel of the Committee on Armed Services, U.S. Government Publishing Office, October 28, 2015b.

U.S. Senate, Is Transition Assistance on Track? Hearing Before the Committee on Veterans' Affairs, U.S. Government Publishing Office, December 15, 2015.

U.S. Senate, *National Defense Authorization Act for Fiscal Year 2017 Report (to Accompany S. 2943)*, U.S. Government Publishing Office, S.R. 114-255, May 18, 2016.

VA—*See* U.S. Department of Veterans Affairs.

Vest, Bonnie M., "Reintegrating National Guard Soldiers After Deployment: Implications and Considerations," *Military Behavioral Health*, Vol. 2, No. 2, 2014.

Werber, Laura, Agnes Gereben Schaefer, Karen Chan Osilla, Elizabeth Wilke, Anny Wong, Joshua Breslau, and Karin E. Kitchens, *Support for the 21st Century Reserve Force: Insights on Facilitating Successful Reintegration for Citizen Warriors and Their Families*, RAND Corporation, RR-206-OSD, 2013. As of September 8, 2022: https://www.rand.org/pubs/research_reports/RR206.html

Werber, Laura, Jennie W. Wenger, Agnes Gereben Schaefer, Lindsay Daugherty, and Mollie Rudnick, *An Assessment of Fiscal Year 2013 Beyond Yellow Ribbon Programs*, RAND Corporation, RR-965-OSD, 2015. As of September 8, 2022: https://www.rand.org/pubs/research_reports/RR965.html

White House, "Joining Forces," webpage, undated. As of February 20, 2023:
https://www.whitehouse.gov/joiningforces/

Wilcox, Sherrie L., Hyunsung Oh, Sarah A. Redmond, Joseph Chicas, Anthony M. Hassan, Pey-Jiuan Lee, and Kathleen Ell, "A Scope of the Problem: Post-Deployment Reintegration Challenges in a National Guard Unit," *Work,* Vol. 50, No. 1, 2015.

Yellow Ribbon Reintegration Program, "About Us," webpage, undated. As of July 7, 2022:
https://www.yellowribbon.mil/cms/about-us/

Yellow Ribbon Reintegration Program, *Fiscal Year 2011: Annual Report to Congress,* Office of the Assistant Secretary of Defense for Reserve Affairs, March 2012.

YRRP—*See* Yellow Ribbon Reintegration Program.